naked
in the
rideshare

naked in the rideshare

(stories of gross miscalculations)

rebecca shaw & ben kronengold

WM

WILLIAM MORROW

An Imprint of HarperCollins*Publishers*

HarperCollins books may be purchased for educational,
business, or sales promotional use. For information, please email
the Special Markets Department at SPsales@harpercollins.com.

FIRST EDITION

Designed by Nancy Singer

Library of Congress Cataloging-in-Publication Data has been
applied for.

ISBN 978-0-06-321578-8

23 24 25 26 27 LBC 5 4 3 2 1

For our grandparents.
(Sorry.)

Contents

College

Post-Grad

Dating

The Real World

The End

introduction

We'd Kill Each Other

For almost as long as we've been dating, we've been writing partners. And over time we've noticed that when people hear we're a couple who works together, they always react the same way: "Oh, my partner and I would kill each other." Always. Whether it's couple friends or parents' friends or siblings who are clearly sleeping together, it's the same shocked expression and four words every time: "We'd kill each other."

So even though we get along just fine, here's what it would look like if a creative disagreement escalated so drastically between us that we, two mildly out-of-shape comedy writers—in good faith—attempted to kill each other.

"Baby?" Ben called out. A chill ran down his spine as he crept into their dimly lit apartment. "Rebecca? Can we talk this out?"

The door slammed behind him. Then—a steel barrel pressed against his back.

"Rebecca?" His voice trembled.

"My therapist told me to apologize less, so I'm not gonna apologize for this. Sorry."

"No!" Ben whipped around and forced her hand to the ceiling. In it, a loaded Glock. *Blam! Blam!* Plaster rained down. Rebecca launched an elbow into Ben's chin. "Agh!" He slid back and spat out what he thought was a tooth (really just an Invisalign attachment).

"So we're doing this, then?" he asked. But he already knew the answer.

Ben tumbled back and ducked behind the Pier One ottoman he'd sworn they didn't need. Hell was he wrong. *Blam! Blam! Blam!* Rebecca walked him down firing bullets, her aim that of someone who'd only shot a gun once at a cousin's wedding, felt weird about it, and then quickly donated to March For Our Lives.

"It's on!" Ben called out, opening a secret compartment in their coffee table. He grabbed a pair of brass knuckles, ready to raise hell.

"WAIT!" Rebecca bellowed. "I'm sorry, did you *build* that secret compartment?"

"Yeah?"

"Oh my God, *whaaat*? Hold on." Rebecca whipped out her phone and dialed. "Mom? So you know how I'm always saying that Ben is surprisingly handy?"

Ben demurred. "I don't know about '*handy*.'"

"He built this, like, compartment thing into our coffee table. No, I know. No, I know! He could've been an engineer. K, gonna kill him now, tell Dad hi!"

Blam!

Another shot blasted the drywall, grazing Ben's one and only "shirt for meetings." He gasped. *Click. Click.* It was Rebecca's last bullet. "Shit."

A smile crept onto Ben's face. "Looks like I've Pier *Won*." He kicked the ottoman into her shins, *really* hoping she'd get the pun but fearing it only really worked in writing. Ben sprang off the ottoman and threw a flying knee into her sternum, then landed on the ground with sheer regret. "Oh my God. Was that not pro-woman?"

Rebecca cocked her head, thinking about it. "No, I think it's, like, equal-opportunity combat?"

"I mean, it seems like in a fourth-wave feminist framework, we're fine?" Ben reasoned. "But maybe problematic considering historic male hegemony?"

"Oh, and also?" Rebecca added.

"Yeah?"

"Suck my dick, bitch." Rebecca pistol-whipped Ben in the face. *Wham!* She tossed him across the kitchen table, then across the dining room table. (It was the same table, plus a small extension Rebecca gingerly unfolded between throws.) Glass shattered across the hardwood floor. Ben cleaned it up immediately.

"That all you got?" Ben tossed away the dustpan, but Rebecca stayed on him. High kick, low kick, low kick, high kick! She was just doing the steps from *A Chorus Line*, but shit was it effective.

Ben slipped into the kitchen, grabbed a knife from the drawer, and lunged—! *Squish*. Rebecca felt a cold crunch against her chest. "Did we—?" Ben looked down. The Styrofoam tip was still on the blade. "Have we never cut anything?!"

Rebecca swung a roundhouse kick, then opened a kitchen

cabinet and smashed a glass bowl onto Ben's skull. *Crash!* Ben tried to do the same, but opened the cabinet for "Paperware and Miscellaneous Foils" instead.

Rebecca fumed. "You should've! Listened! During! The kitchen tour!" She threw a flurry of jabs to the face.

"STOP!" Ben shouted. "I'm sorry, my stomach is *killllling* me."

"Oh my—mine too!" Rebecca gasped. "I bet it was the rock shrimp."

"It must've been, right?!"

It was the delicate dance they do of pretending all ordinary shits stem from extraordinary food poisoning.

"Will you listen to music or something while I . . . ?" Ben trailed off.

"Oh yeah. I was just about to," Rebecca said, mercifully putting her earbuds in.

He went. Then she went. Then he went again.

Then the fight was back on!

Rebecca tossed aside a painting, revealing a secret wall of weapons of her own.

"You haven't Pier Won yet!" she said. (*Yes*, Ben thought. *She* did *get it*.)

Rebecca grabbed a pair of sai from the wall, twirling them around her fingers like the legendary assassin Elektra, if Elektra kept dropping them and saying, "Wait, one more time. Take a video."

"Don't you think those are sorta . . . ?" Ben cringed at the weapons.

"Okay, they're appropriative, right? Because I was afraid they were—"

"I feel like they're borderline?"

"Then you know what? Better safe." Rebecca dropped the sai daggers and canceled herself on Twitter. Fight resumed.

"DIPTYYYYYYQUE!!!" Ben roared, launching Rebecca's candle collection at her, one after another, while she skillfully dodged. He lit the final candle—a $68 Tubéreuse Rebecca pretended was a gift—and sprayed it with some Febreze he'd pocketed during the shit break. Flames raged across the room.

Rebecca arched back, narrowly avoiding the inferno. This bitch had been to Benihana. Then—*zip!*—she launched a grappling gun into the temporary wall behind Ben. She brought it crashing down across his back, shattering the illusion that this was a, quote, "true one-bedroom."

The action that followed didn't so much "happen" as it did "verbally get suggested," as they were both tired and very winded.

Rebecca would kick-step off the wall and land with her legs around Ben's head, the way Scarlett Johansson does in those movies, but more with an eye toward getting eaten out.

Ben would take Rebecca down with his middle school wrestling skills, then remind her again that he did middle school wrestling and that his dad "might still have the footage somewhere." Rebecca would submit out of fear of that becoming her whole day.

Ben would tear their fiddle-leaf fig branch by branch, harming Rebecca far more than any physical pain ever could.

Rebecca would bring up a joke Ben made freshman year of college, suggesting for the first time that it *was* in fact racist. Then she'd use his guilt spiral to land a clean uppercut before admitting that he was "fine" and that Italians are "fair game."

Eventually, they lay in the destruction of their once-nice-ish apartment. Breaths heavy. Bodies broken.

"Why'd it have to come to this?" Ben asked, coughing up blood.

"Because we're a couple," Rebecca said. "And we're in a short story allegorizing society's expectations of how couples fight."

"So true," Ben responded.

"Also, you thought the word was '*end*-dash,' and you kept arguing with me even after I looked it up—"

"It *is* 'end-dash'!"

"It's '*em*-dash'!"

"Not if it's at the end of the sentence—!"

"Fucking die!"

Then they each grabbed a sai dagger and stabbed each other in the heart.

But usually they get along just fine.

childhood

We Have Your Son

SUBJ: **We have your son**
FROM: **[SENDER BLOCKED]**
TO: **Alice and Thatcher Hargrave**

TELL NO ONE YOU HAVE RECEIVED THIS MESSAGE.
DO NOT FORWARD OR SHARE.

We have your son. He is unharmed—*for now*—but if you ever want to
see Harrison again you must follow our instructions exactly. Tomorrow
you will withdraw $5 million in $20 bills from your nearest bank. The
bills must be unmarked or WE WILL KNOW. Once this is completed
you will receive a call on your house phone between 10 and 11 AM
with instructions for the exchange.

Know this: we are but one arm of a global cabal with eyes around the
world. Our reach is wide, and our influence is immeasurable. If you call
the police, or in any way attempt to interfere with us, you will lose your
precious Harrison forever.

Act fast.

—ANONYMOUS

SUBJ: RE: We have your son
FROM: Alice and Thatcher Hargrave
TO: [SENDER BLOCKED]

Keep him!

Best,

Alice and Thatcher Hargrave

SUBJ: RE: RE: We have your son
FROM: [SENDER BLOCKED]
TO: Alice and Thatcher Hargrave

Let us be clear. Unless you comply with our instructions you will never see your son again. There is no organization on Earth that can find him. We will not release Harrison until we have the $5 million in hand.

Respond immediately to confirm that you understand these demands. DO NOT TEST OUR PATIENCE.

—ANONYMOUS

SUBJ: RE: RE: RE: We have your son
FROM: Alice and Thatcher Hargrave
TO: [SENDER BLOCKED]

Totally understand. He's all yours!

Thanks!
Alice and Thatcher

SUBJ: RE: RE: RE: RE: We have your son
FROM: [SENDER BLOCKED]
TO: Alice and Thatcher Hargrave

DO YOU THINK THIS IS A JOKE? Do not make us angry.
Consider this your final warning to comply.

—ANONYMOUS

P.S. Harrison is proving disruptive as a captive. He refuses to cooperate
without phone access. We can't give him his device for obvious reasons,
but we let him watch Bad Bunny's Insta story from afar. Worked for a
while. Advise immediately.

FROM: Alice and Thatcher Hargrave

Sorry for the delay. We went out to dinner last night—first time in
forever. LOL.

re Harrison: teens, right? 😄Not good with downtime. Aim for 6–8
scheduled activities daily (Twitch doesn't count but is a good outlet for
his violent tendencies). Also PSATs are in three months but assume you
guys are taking point now?? Thanks so much!

All the best,
Alice and Thatcher

FROM: [SENDER BLOCKED]

We are growing WEARY OF THIS. If the ransom is not paid in 24 hours, we will begin to cut off Harrison's fingers, starting with the ones he says he needs for piano lessons. Their is no other way.

FROM: Alice and Thatcher Hargrave

Haaa! Tell him he plateaued in piano years ago.

Also—*There* is no other way. (PSATs)

Worried for you guys,
Alice and Thatcher

FROM: [SENDER BLOCKED]

We are lowering the ransom to 4 million. Really, anywhere in the 3–4 million range will be fine.

NOW LISTEN CLOSELY. What's the deal with his food restrictions? Are these real or is he fucking with us? I've never heard of an "oil intolerance"/can't find anything about it online.

Thanks,
Anonymous

FROM: Alice and Thatcher Hargrave

Oil intolerance is unfortunately real. If he's telling you he's vegan, though, he just decided that on Wednesday, so don't stress too much. We just lie and tell him we're serving Impossible meat. LOL.

Btw he's on this kick about growing out his hair lately. Just let him do it. College interviews aren't until the fall, at which point CUT IT WITHOUT QUESTION. He'll say it's an "aesthetic identity." Just tune out. Maybe tie him up? Assume you have ropes, zip ties, etc.

FROM: [SENDER BLOCKED]

Harrison won't take his Accutane. Instead he's trying some skin-care routine he saw on 4chan, and now he has a rash and his shits smell terrible.

Still have not heard from you about ransom. 2 mil sound okay? Please respond soon. Thx

FROM: [AUTOMATIC RESPONSE] Alice and Thatcher Hargrave

Aloha!

If you're receiving this message, the Hargraves are away from their computers. We're spending the next week on a long-overdue Lanai vacation with limited access to email. Please direct all urgent messages to our household manager, Danielle [HargraveAsst@gmail.com]. Hope you're having a peaceful summer!

xx
Alice and Thatcher

TO: HargraveAsst@gmail.com
FROM: [SENDER BLOCKED]

Hi Danielle, it's us (we kidnapped Harrison, not sure if the Hargraves have mentioned). Hope you're doing well.

We're just following up on the below messages to the Hargraves. Can you please ask them to contact us as soon as they can? Also Harrison said we need to pick up his prescription. What is Zoloftolax???

Nice to e-meet,
Anonymous

TO: [SENDER BLOCKED]
FROM: HargraveAsst@gmail.com

Hi guys,

So sorry, the Hargraves say they'll get in touch when they get back.

TO: HargraveAsst@gmail.com
FROM: [SENDER BLOCKED]

Any word? It's been ten days.

TO: HargraveAsst@gmail.com
FROM: [SENDER BLOCKED]

Hello?????

FROM: Alice and Thatcher Hargrave

Sorry, team! Just touched down a couple days ago and this was stuck in the email backlog. Feels like we need another vacation already, ha!

Politely passing on 2 million. For that amount you should've kidnapped our daughter Lily, 7 y/o. She's an angel. 😇

How's Harrison?

—A + T

FROM: JosephKinzington@gmail.com

Not great!!!! He's been writing song parodies about the political climate and trying them out on us. When we didn't "clap like we meant it" he said "art is dead" and threatened to cut off his OWN FINGERS. Then he laughed and said, "It's a vibe." We cannot emphasize enough, your child is broken.

Please write back soon with plans to take him back. Half a mil would suffice.

FROM: [SENDER BLOCKED]

PLEASE DISREGARD LAST EMAIL. SENT FROM WRONG ADDRESS

FROM: Alice and Thatcher Hargrave

No worries, we're not looking into it!

Bummer about Harrison. Sounds like a phase? We love our son, but honestly we don't half-a-mil love him?? If that makes sense??

FROM: [SENDER BLOCKED]

250k.

FROM: Alice and Thatcher Hargrave

No deal.

FROM: [SENDER BLOCKED]

90k.

FROM: Alice and Thatcher Hargrave

Respectfully decline. Thanks!

FROM: [SENDER BLOCKED]

WE WILL PAY YOU.

FROM: Alice and Thatcher Hargrave

. . . Is it bad if we say no?

FROM: [SENDER BLOCKED]

YES IT'S BAD.

FROM: Alice and Thatcher Hargrave

Give us a little time to chew it over. Thanks so much!

FROM: [SENDER BLOCKED]

Dear Alice and Thatcher,

We hope you've had a nice summer. Danielle says you're in Morocco now? Sounds fun.

We're reaching out because things are looking up here. Your son turns out to be a pretty cool kid, especially once we gave him his phone back. (He explained he wouldn't call the cops/thinks they shouldn't exist.) He's been showing us some pretty hilarious videos on TikTok, and we showed him *Seinfeld*, which he says isn't as "shit-boring" as he thought. It's been sort of nice watching a kid who genuinely feels his feelings. Hell, he's even helped us understand ours too. We do "vibe checks" once a week now. Today was a grumpy day, but that's okay because we're giving each other space to decompress.

Anyway, just wanted to say thanks. See attached photo of us across state lines—sorry about the pierced ear, but at least it's still attached to his head, ya know?

All the best,
Joe and Ralph

P.S. Gonna forward a clip of his new voting-rights song parody. Harrison says it still needs mastering, but honestly we're pretty proud.

FROM: Harrison.Hargrave@gmail.com
TO: Alice and Thatcher Hargrave

Mom and dad, what's my SoundCloud password? Respond immediately. DO NOT TEST MY PATIENCE.

^Joe and Ralph taught me that.

Eustace, 1 Through 84

Throughout his entire life, Eustace McDuff's hair was invariably pubey. Somewhere between Art Garfunkel at Central Park and Justin Timberlake circa 2002. Some things are important to know because they come back later in the story. This, in the spirit of honesty, is not one of those things.

Day One

"Checking in?"

Across the desk, a young man lifted his head. He wasn't sure how he got here, nor did he remember waiting in the sprawling line behind him. Instead, he moved with the kind of floaty acceptance you would in a dream.

"Eustace McDuff," he replied, his voice ping-ponging through the corridor.

"No kidding, kid," the man behind the desk answered. "We're all Eustace McDuff."

Faces are a funny thing. If Eustace had paid closer attention, he might have noticed that everyone around him shared his same one.

His same bushy brow and sunken eyes, his sharp jaw and forgettable, bad lips. But as much as his focus would allow, Eustace had been more taken by his surroundings.

The deluge of Eustaces—of all different ages—filed through long, antiseptic hallways. Gleaming white walls with rounded corners, like the silicone mold of a hallway rather than a hallway itself. Finally a main greeting area, ovular and grand, with large portholes. And just out those windows: the cosmos. An endless swirl of light pinks and greens and blues. The soft, pastel palette you'd hope to find at the end of the universe. Still in a trance, Eustace processed all this like a computer identifying a cat: numerically, without judgment. "That is a cat."

"Step forward, kid." Eustace—our Eustace—was still milling about the check-in counter. "State your age."

"Just turned fourteen." Eustace walked under a sleek, white door frame. Notches on the side marked E.M. 13 Y/O, E.M. 14 Y/O, E.M. 15 Y/O, and so on.

"Stand up tall. Back against the post."

Eustace's height matched the 14 Y/O marking. And suddenly, a soft *ping* of approval.

"Welcome to the symposium, 14." Then Eustace joined a crowd of himself.

Now by anyone's standards, Eustace had been going through a lot at fourteen. His parents' divorce had just been finalized, a douse of peroxide on a blistering, four-year-old wound. Meanwhile in school, the kids were splitting off, as they tend to do at that age, into the academically remarkable and unremarkable; Eustace was somewhat surprised to find himself in the second camp. And then there were the urges. Not the typical pubescent urges that emerged a few years earlier, but a newer, deeper yearning to be free from himself. Eustace wanted to get out of his own head, or his own way, or something. His friend Davis from AV Club suggested that was called "getting drunk," but Davis had neither been drunk nor could help them get drunk, so they just went back to playing *Soulcalibur.*

All in all, it was a great time for the universe to plop "14" into an intergenerational summit with his various selves. And as Eustace came out of his dreamlike state, blinking hard atop a set of Escher stairs, he started to notice the signage around him: posters emblazoned with phrases like GET TO KNOW YOURSELF and A LIFETIME OF EUSTACE. If this truly *was* a conference of different Eustaces, 14 reasoned, it could be a great opportunity. He could have some of his most pressing questions answered. He could get a glimpse into his future, the man he'd become, and what books, if any, he'd read one day. But as soon as the excitement came, it went. A sign on a doorway in front of him read EUSTACE, AGES 10–15. In finer print: TWEEN COMMISSION. It was a goddamn subcommittee.

The sight beyond the doorway made 14's gut wrench. His eleven-year-old self thumbed his palate expander at a conference table, while across the way, thirteen-year-old Eustace practiced the fast part of Estelle's "American Boy" loudly enough so everyone could hear. Worst of all was 10, the youngest in the room. 10 was staring right back at our Eustace, waving wildly like the kid who skipped two grades and now needed friends in pre-calc. To 14, the earnestness was visceral.

"Twenties right this way! Welcome to the best five days of our life!"

14's ears perked up. Behind him, the twenties were filing into their *own* conference room. A promised land of sideburns and vodka funk. 14's heart raced. And then suddenly, he was making a break for it. He barreled toward the twenties' room. Feet away. Then inches. Then—

"Actually . . ." A figure stepped into 14's path. "We teens and tweens are in Room D." The figure across from him *was* 14. Practically him, at least, separated by just a razor nick on his neck and all the confidence that comes with having a razor nick on one's neck.

"15." The other Eustace tapped an ID badge. "I cut myself shaving."

In the hours that followed, the universe gave 14 exactly what he didn't want: more of himself. Selves he'd already grown out of. 12 had a lot of questions about masturbation. 13 had a lot of answers. And when our Eustace tried baiting 15 into revealing the Clippers' record next season, 15 just spewed some holier-than-thou garbage about how these five days are about "reflecting on the past, not commenting on the future." 14 worried he too would become that insufferable one day when given a small amount of power. But mostly he just worried 15's body wasn't radically hotter than his own.

"So does our Ab Blaster break, or . . . ?"

"Not here to comment on the future," 15 said paunchily. "But, y—yes. It breaks."

Day Two

In the cosmic void of space-time, lunch is self-serve. Specifically, Eustaces serve other Eustaces. On his second day at the symposium, 14 perused the food options: grilled salmon, grilled corn, grilled peppers.

"God, leave it to the forty-somethings." From up the line, 22 snarked at the line cooks, "Nice work, boys. I was worried we wouldn't have a grilling phase."

"Ignore him," 23 called out beside him. "He's in his early twenties. He'd kill for a hobby."

"You're only a year older," 22 shot back.

"Yeah, but I found knitting."

"You did?"

"Yes, dude!"

"We knit?!"

"Hell yes!" 22 and 23 said, synchronized.

14 smiled from down the line. His mind buzzed. How and when does he become *them*?

14 plunked the nearest grilled corn onto his tray and tailed the pair, a three-top table in his sights. Then a small voice startled him.

"We're prolly in a pocket dimension." 14 whipped left to see 10, the youngest of the tween committee, staring up at him. "That's my theory, at least. A pocket dimension. Or a dream, prolly."

14 nodded vacantly, eyes still fixed on the older kids.

"What do you think?" 10 asked. He had the anxious habit of brushing his tongue across his teeth idly. It made 14 nervous. Specifically, it made him brush his tongue across his teeth idly.

"I think you're onto something, bud." 14 tried on a hokey camp-counselor voice. "Why don't you let me know how that theory . . . like, evolves and stuff." Then 14 turned away and beelined for the three-top.

"So you're sitting—? With them? Okay, roger that!" 10 called out. Then more tongue-to-teeth madness.

"So this week's fucking weird, huh?" 14 took a seat at the twenties' table, coming in hot.

23 chewed a grilled pepper, heavy-lidded. He turned to 22. "Did we always curse like that?"

"It sounded forced, right?"

"Like someone was making him say it."

"Or like he heard it in a Kings of Leon song. Kings of Leon? Is that right?"

"I dunno. I can't keep up with kids ten years ago."

22 and 23 were practically identical, speaking with one hazy mind. The only way to tell them apart, besides the ID badges hanging around their necks, was that 23 had hair connecting his beard to his mustache. 22 stared at these hair bridges enviously and often.

"Anyway, Teen Beat," 22 went on, "rules say you can only sit with your decade." He gestured around the room. Next to them, a table of younger Eustaces were scribbling in coloring books.

"Oh, sorry." 14 reddened and stood up. "I didn't know there were rules."

"Neither did we."

"Nonsense, right?" 23 grabbed 14's ID badge, *zipped* it out toward them, and pulled 14 back into his seat. Then a collective "Oof!"

"Oh, *shit*."

"*You're* fourteen?" They studied the badge.

"Yeah . . . Why?" 14 worried. "Does—something bad happen?"

"No . . ."

"No, all the bad stuff is already *happening*," 22 answered.

14 sat with this. Even by a lifetime's standards, he was the "oof." He rolled the corn around his tray.

"Let me guess." 23 kept chewing. "Not having fun at the narcissism conference?"

14 forced a smile. "Yeah, I don't—my age group is just, like, all divorce and porn recommendations. And I thought this could

be a chance to figure things out, but . . . I'm starting to think that won't happen."

The older Eustaces glanced at each other, a glint of pity in their eyes. Then the pity turned to mischief.

"You know, you seem like a good kid."

"Good, not great."

"We remember."

"We were there."

"So . . . Here's what we're gonna do." 23 reached back and grabbed a fistful of colored pencils from the kids' table. A cacophony of moans and shouts of "doodiehead" from 5 through 7.

"You know your group leader, 15? Total dick, by the way. Don't turn fifteen," 23 said.

"Okay . . ."

"See, the 'fivers' have special privileges. They run the show here. They can go anywhere . . . talk to anyone . . ."

They grabbed 14's badge again and scratched away at it with the colored pencils.

"Well, now *you*," 23 went on, "have those privileges." He placed the badge back on the table. With the help of a black colored pencil, *14* now read *15*. Somewhat sloppily, but good enough at a glance.

"Wait. You guys can do that?!" 14 asked.

"Fuck no!" 23 answered. "That's how you curse, by the way."

"See how it just rolled off the tongue?"

"Anyway, ya crazy kid"—23 slid over the badge—"take this and go wild."

"Wild how?" 14 asked.

22 just smiled. "There are answers in this circle jerk, Twino-thée Chalamet," he said. "If you really want them, you just need to find the you who has them."

23 offered jazz fingers. "The Eustace of all Eustaces," he said with feigned melodrama.

14's thoughts raced. *The Eustace of all Eustaces*. He stared down at his forged badge, reeling from his new power. His new purpose.

22 and 23 went back to eating their lunches. A quiet moment passed.

"So anyway, we're thinking of doing each other."

"Oh, that's . . . nice."

Day Three

14's world had been cracked open. What so far had felt like a stuffy, corporate retreat in the clouds suddenly became his very own existential ops mission: find the Eustace of all Eustaces, get answers—*real* answers—about their life, and, most importantly, skip over this crappy, cosmic "oof" of an adolescence. But which Eustace was he looking for?

Unfortunately for 14, the symposium seemed infinite in size—a labyrinth of halls and doorways, signs and corridors. 14's first stop with his new access was the nursery. He hadn't been trying to go to the nursery, per se. Instead, he'd taken an admittedly pervy turn at BREASTFEEDING and just happened to stumble upon it. And there, behind a large, spotless window, he watched Eustaces aged 1–4 brought through the motions of infancy.

2 stirred in a crib. 1 dozed in a bassinet while a sleek robotic arm nursed him with a synthetic breast. 14 couldn't help but feel like 12 would be interested in this breast, and he made a mental note to take him back here later. Then he got distracted because 3 crapped in 4's hands.

"Be honest. Was there a cuter kid than us?" A few feet away, a middle-aged Eustace admired the scene, scratching his head on the bald spot.

"Oh. Yeah. I'm pretty sure not," 14 answered.

"Well, hey, Pretty Sure Not. I'm 55." He reached out his hand. "Stupid. That was stupid."

"Oh. Hi. I'm fourt—"

"15. I know. Saw the badge."

Our Eustace swallowed hard and nodded.

"So we both playing hooky today?" 55 asked. "Yeah, the fifties will talk your ear off. I've been 'in the bathroom' for an hour now. But I'll tell you, they're a smart bunch."

14 turned back to the nursery window, a polite exit. But the words lingered with him. "Are we?" He glanced back at 55. "A smart bunch?"

Then a knowing smile spread across 55's forgettable, bad lips.

"It's called La Galleria Eustace," 55's voice rang through a marble museum wing. "That's what I call it, anyway. No one knows what anything's called here. Or how any of us got here." He eyed 14 suspiciously. "Do you know how we got here?"

14 shook his head.

"Figured. Just checking."

All around them, an endless maze of white walls boasted gorgeous, golden frames. Rows and rows of drawings. And in the drawings . . . ducks. Some cows too, and one deformed hand-turkey. The painted, polka-dotted creatures of an American childhood. So abstract, in fact, that if they weren't signed *Eustace, age 5, age 6*, and so forth on the bottom, they might have sold for a large sum of money to some very rich, confused Scandinavians. But instead they hung here, with no monetary value, an early retrospective of Eustace's creative life.

14 saw the narrative coming a mile away. As the construction-paper drawings turned to papier-mâché turned to notebook doodles, 14 was growing more and more certain of why 55 brought him to the gallery. Eustace may not have been "smart" in the traditional sense. But he—just to skip the long walk here—was, very likely, increasingly definitely the artistic mind of his generation. Like any child of divorce or male generally, he'd deep down always suspected this might be the case.

14 browsed around for twenty minutes. Then twenty more. But strangely enough, nothing on the walls showed signs of artistic genius. He studied the knitting phase sparked by 23. He

revisited the blocky *S* doodles that consumed his early tween period. But there were no marks of a creative visionary. Barely marks of creative vision.

"Come look at this," 55 called out. 14 followed, anxious to find his magnum opus. Instead, just a handmade birthday card floating in a glass frame. It read, *Happy Bird-Day, Cheryl*.

"She was an admin at our first job. Loved parakeets." 55 stared with almost the same adoration he did at the nursery. "One year in our thirties, we started making these for everyone at work. By hand. Always with some personalized joke about them. About their hobbies, their kids, or what have you."

"And this is . . . good?" 14 studied the card's crude construction.

"Oh no. They get better. Never great, though," 55 explained. "*But* . . . we become the youngest manager at our company."

14's head cocked.

"A good manager too. People *really* like us. And we keep making these"—55 motioned to an entire wall of birthday cards—"at our next company. And the next one. And even the one we start ourselv—" 55 caught himself. "Whoop. Well, now I'm saying too much."

For the first time all week, 14 felt something. Something close to excitement. A sense of hope for what was to come.

"School is . . . a very specific kind of smart, kid." 55 put his hand on 14's shoulder. "We're *people* people, you and I."

14 held back a smile.

"You and me?" 55 questioned himself. "You and I? Yeah, we never do great at grammar." Then 55 sauntered off down the gallery.

Day Four

The next day, 14 arrived laser-focused. If 55 could put him at ease about one problem, one nagging insecurity, imagine what an even older Eustace could do. The oldest Eustace, who had lived through it all already. The *Eustace of all Eustaces*.

But now 14 was on the clock. He had just two days left to get his answers. On the divorce. On how it would impact his life. On this inescapable feeling that he wanted to be someone else, anyone else. Fortunately for 14, a half day of searching led him to where he wanted to be: a velvet double door in the heart of the symposium.

WELCOME, a golden plaque read, EUSTACE 80–87.

Knock. Knock. Knock.

At the end of life, there's a movie theater. A select few octogenarian Eustaces sat in leather lift seats. A support staff of late-sixty- and -seventy-somethings buzzed around them.

In the back, 14 collected himself. Then he began a morbid game of Which Eustace Looks Like He's About to Kick It? The trick, he quickly discovered, was to follow the coughs.

"Hi," 14 said in a hushed voice, taking a seat beside an older, practically all-phlegm Eustace. "You must be the oldest me."

The old man hacked away in his seat. "I'm just choking on a kernel, ya jackass!" he croaked. "You're looking for 87!"

"Who is?!" an even hoarser voice called out from the back.

"There's another kid here to suck wisdom out your catheter, Gramps!" All the octogenarians cracked up in laughter.

"Christ's sake. Up here, kid!" the voice yelled back. "Plenty of knowledge left to piss out!" Then more laughs as 14, utterly outside of the joke, floated up the aisle to finally find *him*. The Eustace of all Eustac—

"Nip twist!" 87 grabbed 14's chest and wrenched.

"Ow!"

"Loser says what?"

"What?"

"Ha! We've been watching footage of 9 all day. That kid had a hell of a time."

14 glanced up at the big screen. On it, memories from his life played in crisp, clear color. Mostly memories he hadn't even made yet.

"You seen this?" 87 motioned toward the screen with a liver-spotted hand. "It's mainly shits, sleeps, and showers. But they'll scrub through to get to the good stuff."

"Wow. That must be really specia—"

"Valentine's Day '34!" 87 called out. A roar of applause filled the room. "Give the people what they want!" he yelled toward the projectionist.

14 waited out the clamor. "If you have a second, sir. Should I call you 'sir'?"

"Go on already!"

"Okay . . ." 14 took a breath. "I guess . . . So, I'm fourteen. And I've been told a lot of the crappy stuff that happens to us is happening to *me*. Right now. Well, I guess I know it is. Because I'm going through it—"

"Before I'm dead, maybe?!"

"Sorry. I'm—just, I'm tired of it! I'm sick of myself, I guess. I'm sick of, like, *us*. I'm sick of *being us*." The words poured out, and with them, a deeper kind of sadness sank in.

"Sick of *us*?" 87 laughed back. "Ha! Kid. You and I are not the same person."

14's face contorted. "We are, though. That's, like, the whole point."

"Yeah? You think we're the same? Okay. How many times have you been married?"

14 bristled. "Well, none."

"Twice." 87 held up two fingers. "How many times you have sex in the back of a car?"

"None?"

"*Eight* times." 87 pointed at himself. "Two of them moving. How many years you spend in college? How many kids you got? Grandkids? How many bad film classes have you sat through at the Y? Or sips of whiskey you've taken that you've *actually* enjoyed?"

14 just sat there, his head vaguely shaking side to side.

"You're not sick of you, kid. You're sick of the moment you're in." 87 stared into his younger eyes. "Believe me. There will be plenty more of 'em." Then 87 looked back up at the theater screen. 14 followed his gaze. More shits, sleeps, and showers, naturally. But also . . . weddings, meetings, dances, dinners, births, hikes, funerals, first dates, and one surprising, late-in-life bris.

"It's the end-of-history illusion," 87 said, raising his eyebrows theatrically. "That's what they call it, anyway. We all think that who we are right now is who we'll always be." 87 lifted a soda cup, handed it to 14. "But at the end of the day . . ." 14 sipped. Pure whiskey.

"Gah! That is *awful*."

". . . You're not you yet, kid." 87 winked and enjoyed a sip himself.

14 sat in the movie theater for the rest of the day. Hours and hours and hours. He thought about 87's words. And as he processed, he watched the film, filtering through the hikes and meetings for something that might make sense to him. The outcome of his parents' divorce, how high school would end up . . . But he never got those answers.

Instead, the only memory that stood out was that of a ten-year-old boy in the back of a car, his parents arguing from the front seat. It was a family trip that they'd abandon halfway through. 14

wasn't that kid on screen anymore. He felt lucky for it. He felt even luckier that he knew where to find him.

Day Five

"You immature little douche!" 15 rushed 14 in the cafeteria. "You know how irresponsible it is to disappear for three days—?"

"15? Real quick, before you start?"

"What?"

"Screw you." Then 14 strolled right past him, tray in hand.

"'Screw you'? Really? I *am* you!"

"Then screw me, I guess! Screw me *and* you!"

"Hey, Jizzney Channel! How'd it go?!" 22 shouted from his three-top table.

"You find him?" 23 called out. "The Eustace of all Eustaces?"

14 flashed a thumbs-up.

"Yes, dude! Did he help you?"

"He's about to!" 14 kept walking. "We're about to help each other, actually."

22 and 23's brows furrowed. They tracked 14's stride as he crossed the cafeteria and found a familiar face.

"Hey!"

"Oh. Hi, 14!" 10 looked up from his tray of food. "You're back?"

"I . . . think I am now. Yeah." 14 smiled and took the empty seat beside 10. He cut into his grilled salmon and spoke with a mouth half-full. "Hey, crazy idea?"

"Yeah?"

"Do you want to spend the day together?" 14 asked.

10 lit up. "Like, me and you?" he replied. "Sure! We can walk back to the conference room together prolly—"

"No, I was thinking more like . . ." 14 interrupted. "Well, it's our last day and whatever. I was thinking we could just wander. And talk."

"Oh! That'd be good!" 10 smiled.

"Right? Okay, good!" They dug into their lunches, reflecting Xeroxed smiles. "You know, there's this synthetic boob I found, if you want to go see that."

"Oh, no thanks! I'm good."

"Great." 14 smiled wider. "We'll find something else, then."

Alexander and the Terrible, Horrible, No Good, Very Bad Day That Was Made Better by White Privilege

I went to sleep with gum in my mouth and then I woke up with gum in my hair and also a sense of relief that I'm not the target of an oppressive criminal justice system. But still, I had gum in my hair. That's when I knew it'd be a terrible, horrible, no good, very bad day.

At breakfast, my brother Anthony found a Corvette Sting Ray race car in his cereal box, and Nick found a Junior Undercover Agent code ring in his cereal box, but I didn't get any prize in my cereal box except for the forever prize of not having to think about the color of my skin on a daily basis. But I would've liked a race car. Chalk it up to my terrible, horrible, no good, very bad day.

At school, Mrs. Dickens said I sang too loud during music

class. This made me feel terrible and horrible. I felt even worse when I remembered that the indie-pop EP I would one day release via my family's music connections was still years away. Aw brother. As if my day wasn't terrible enough already.

At snack time, I opened my lunch box to find lima beans. I hate lima beans. My mom packs my lunch because she can afford to stay home since she has benefitted from generations of well-compensated employment. But lima beans? Screw you, Mom!

At the bus stop, I by mistake whistled at a girl, and she stormed over to me all red in the face. But then she became my girlfriend. We went to her house, and her parents immediately accepted me as one of their own. They offered me a high-level job at their family business, but I said I didn't need it. Then I said I had to leave because I was in the middle of my terrible, horrible, no good, very bad daaaayugh.

Then I went to the bank and wandered into a vault. The security guard ran up to me, which is so typical given the day I was having. But instead of getting me in trouble, he gave me a free TD Bank visor and asked if I wanted to see one hundred hundred-dollar bills. The money was okay, I guess. But it still wasn't cool enough to change my Terrible. Horrible. No good. Very bad. Day.

Then I went to city hall and submitted paperwork to run for public office. It was easy, really. I just told people I would get rid of things I never used before, like Social Security and Medicaid, and they signed my petition. It wasn't hard to fund my campaign either, since it turns out everyone I know also benefits from generations of well-compensated employment. But then, out of the blue, all these mean people online started saying bad things about me. Ugh. Of course they'd do that on my terrible, horrible, no good, very bad day.

I had to get away, so I Ubered to the airport and got on a plane. That was easy too. I just told TSA I lost my passport and they said, "No problem, sir. Right this way." Once we boarded, I went into the cockpit and threatened the pilot so that he'd reroute the flight to Australia. "I think I'd like it there," I said. But by the time we landed in Perth, there were police officers waiting for me. *Oh, great*, I thought. Just when I thought my day couldn't get worse.

Then while I was in custody waiting for my mom to pick me up, the police officers served me dinner. Grilled cheese with lima beans. Perfect. Just the perfect way to cap my terrible, horrible, no good, very bad day.

Anyway, my agent just told me I got a book deal. Maybe tomorrow will be better.

Report Cards
for 25-Year-Olds

Growing up, we were what you'd describe as "good kids." We listened in class, we were usually the teacher's pet, and we genuinely loved learning. But now we're twenty-five, and we're tired and we're high and we hate the gym. So to give you a sense of just how much we've changed—and, even worse, not changed—here are our actual kindergarten report cards, *along with some honest assessments of what we're like now at twenty-five. Please refrain from judgment. Or judge. We're too tired to push back.*

Acclimation

Age 5

"Ben is a sheer joy to have in class. He has transitioned with minimal issues into his kindergarten life. He arrives each morning ready to begin his day. Around the classroom, Ben is best described as a naturally inquisitive boy who is interested in knowing the 'how' and 'why' of many things. It always makes us smile."

Age 25

"Ben is a tiny nightmare to have in the apartment. He has transitioned with many issues into his twenty-something life. He wakes up each morning with a start, bursting out of a fever dream in which Samantha Bee asked him to write a joke on abortion and he took it too far. Around the apartment, Ben is best described as a naturally confused caveman who is interested in knowing the 'where' and 'where' of many things, e.g., 'Where's the salt?' 'Where's the pepper?' and 'Wait, babe, where's the salt?' It's always right in front of him."

Mathematics

Age 5

"Rebecca uses math throughout the day in a variety of activities. Whether it's detecting number patterns, exploring expanded notation, or mastering addition and subtraction, mathematics is a cornerstone of Rebecca's academic life."

Age 25

"Rebecca uses math once a month and it's to figure out the tip and she always gets it wrong and she has to call the restaurant after."

Reading

Age 5

"Throughout the semester, Ben has emerged as a skilled early reader.

This quarter we have been working on letter recognition and rhyming words. Continued hours spent reading books at home may result in strengthening his literacy skills further. Some of his favorites include *The Rainbow Fish* and *The Giving Tree*."

Age 25

"Throughout the last sixty-four semesters, Ben has not read one full book cover to cover. Ben has barely even read his own book cover to cover, and he wrote it. Continued hours spent watching Marvel breakdowns and porn at home may result in early brain atrophy. Some of his favorites include *47 Details You Missed in Thor Ragnarok* and *Miami Blowbang 9*."

Vocabulary

Age 5

"Rebecca's advanced vocabulary has become a pillar of her learning experience. She has incorporated words such as 'situation,' 'grasp,' and even 'paradigm' into her in-class writing, much to the delight of her teachers. We can't wait to see where this love of language takes her next!"

Age 25

"Rebecca's love of language took her into a career of dick jokes. She has incorporated words such as 'nutting,' 'fistable,' and even 'smegma' into her scripts, much to the disgust of her agents. We can't wait to see what smutty corner of a women's prison this love of language takes her to next!"

Jobs & Chores

Age 5

"Ben is very responsible when it comes to his chores. Whether he is Math Magician or Mood Meter Master, Ben has a special way of getting his task done and doing it well! We are staggered by his diligence. Go, Ben!"

Age 25

"Ben is very responsible when it comes to his chores *until you look even slightly closely.* Whether he is Dish Cleaner or Fridge Organizer, Ben has a special way of looking like he is doing the work without actually doing anything. We are staggered by his ability to hem and haw until someone else does the task for him. Clean up the fucking fridge, Ben!"

Social Skills

Age 5

"We are thrilled to report that Rebecca is making friends within the classroom. Her many fine qualities make her an ideal classmate and compassionate friend. We're confident her eagerness for community and connection will stay with her always."

Age 25

"Yeah, so Rebecca's closed for business. After twenty years of community and connection and whatever, Rebecca has what can only be described as 'medical-grade social burnout.' Rebecca's friends are her plants, and she is not available for dinner this Friday."

Snack Time

Age 5

"Ben does not like his foods touching. While this may sound concerning, we chalk this up to five-year-old 'growing pains' and are confident this will work itself out over time!"

Age 25

"Ben does not like his foods touching. While this may sound concerning, it also *is* concerning. We chalk this up to twenty-five-year-old 'mental health issues' and are confident this will be the rest of his life, so ahhhhhh!!!"

Ethics & Moral Code

Age 5

"Rebecca is not one to take shortcuts. Whether it's staying quiet during Silent Rest Time or enforcing the 'work by yourself' structure of certain individual projects, Rebecca's honest nature and understanding of rules shine through in her actions."

Age 25

"Rebecca's going to hell. Plain and simple. She has a recycling bin that she doesn't use. She faked Covid to get out of a birthday dinner. She once started training for a race to raise money for cystic fibrosis but quit when it got 'hot out' and told everyone the race was canceled. Not sure what all that narc shit in kindergarten was about, but yeah, she's roasting in a big way."

Spelling

Age 5

"Ben's spelling is quite good, and he spaces between words beautifully. Take this journal entry about Field Day on May 2 when Ben wrote: 'My favorite activty (activity) was the 25 yard rase (race).'"

Age 25

"Ben's spelling peaked in high school, and then dropped precipitously somewhere around 22 or 23, as if someone hit him in the head with a non-English dictionary. Take this text message to Rebecca on January 18 when Ben wrote: 'The refridgerdoor (refrigerator) smells like parlsy (parsley) but I can't find the parlsy (parsley) anywere (anywhere).' It was right in front of him."

teenage years

Letters from Color War

My Dearest Mother,

I pen this letter on the eve of the 6th of August, the ghastliest day of my short life. We were roused to the sound of horns, as colored smoke filled the air. Blue first, then red. We choked on the acrid taste, driving us from the cabins and toward the upper field. And then, dear Mother, it began. A soul-curdling screech ripped through the skies as *NSYNC's Lance Bass hurdled down the zipline. A banner unfurled behind him. Emblazoned upon it, rippling in the cold morning air: CAMP BRYN LAKE FOR GIRLS - COLOR WAR 2023. We were left with but one haunting question: "Who is that man, and why is he not Migos?"

∽

7 August. The first day of combat. Our troops stood battle-ready thanks to a supply of blue Converse from Sadie Katz's mother, who overnighted them from a Lester's in Rye Brook.

At 11 o'clock, we were instructed to compose parody songs. For nearly an hour, Mother, it was Hell upon this earth. Titles were suggested and summarily shot down. "I'm a Blueliever"—a failed endeavor. "Wake Me Up Before Blue Go-Go"—dead upon arrival. Verily, artists were dropping left and right. Bieber was "overdone"; Dr. Dre "didn't slap." Bon Jovi was suggested, but no one could remember if he'd been canceled or was just from New Jersey. Ultimately, the troops rallied around "I Don't Know About You, But I'm Feeling Blu-u-ue." Inform Papa that it was a decisive victory, Mother. A swift triumph, marred only by the shrieks of Dani Markowitz as she got her very first period mid-chorus. I don't know about you, dear Mother, but on this day, I'm feeling blu-u-ue.

∽

My dearest family, I write to you as we take respite in the bunk, as is required from 12:30 to 1:15 so the gingers don't burn. In these quiet moments, thoughts turn often to our boys back home. I wonder if Michael's voice has dropped, or if Graham R. has perfected his Stewie impression. Fortunately for me, I keep a yearbook with their round, pocked faces nearby so the girls from LA can be mean about middle-class boys. Still, I will dream of Graham R. on this night and all nights, and not of Jenna Rosen's story about rubbing V to P with Tom Holland at her dad's Oscars party. That's all for now, Mother. The gaga pits beckon.

⌁

Dusk has fallen. All the grass is trodden into the earth. The cabins lay battered with Silly String after a long day's fight. And above it all hangs Lance Bass, our silent judge. You see, on that fateful morn, his harness became so entangled with the Color War banner that there was deemed no safe way to lower him down. In poorer fortune still, his rescue was stalled when the fire department was rerouted to Camp Pontiac, where an illicit doobie had set a dance pavilion ablaze. So till his moment comes, Lance Bass watches us all. Noiselessly, his spirits broken, sipping on a Capri Sun the counselors tossed up to him hours ago. He takes in the wreckage like the eyes of God himself. He calls hoarsely for his manager. There is no manager in sight.

⌁

Ambush! Our platoon was traversing home from pajama brunch when a dozen fighters sprung from the trees. E.G.G.s knocked down our first line. (Eggs.) I dodged water balloon upon water balloon, but many of my companions were not so lucky and had their tits seen through their shirts. "Those bitches got me!" cried Riley Shelby-Newman, cradling her chest. I'd barely turned around to see another balloon hit her in the back of the head, sending her retainer flying toward the ropes course. Now, finally, it is quiet once more. We tend to the wounded and plot our revenge. Mother, if this letter makes it to you, do send me a pair of jeans with candy stuffed in the pockets. And a gun. I think I would do well with a gun here.

∽

K, so our revenge is gonna happen later. It's a rain day, so we're all staying inside and watching *Freaky Friday* or whatever. War starts again tomorrow. Tell Dad hiiiii.

∽

10 August. The rain lifted, and with it our cease-fire. Red co-captain Skylar DeNilo was caught rubbing her plantar wart on Blue's pillows during lunchtime. The counselors took pity on young Skylar, for she's a "good kid" and a "child of divorce starting last week but don't tell her yet she doesn't know." On this eve, we sit with the older girls of the Blue barracks and share stories and learn curse words. Some of the curse words are jokey and fine, but some others are unspeakable. I must admit I forgot which ones are which. Nevertheless, I pray this missive reaches you, Mother. We are truly in the heart of battle, but we will get those cunts.

∽

Troubling news from the front. In the opening moments of Capture the Flag, our compatriot Elana Harlow caught a forearm to the face from the enemy team. She is dead now,

Mother. Socially, that is, as her face is all puffy and she cannot attend canteen tonight. Fortunately for the loyal Blue, the infirmary ruled it a mere broken nose. She expects to make a full recovery but says to "not be shocked if the surgeon has to, like, make it totally different." Now all the girls in camp want to break their noses for the cause, dear Mother. And that, I must say, is a heartening sight.

∽

13 August. The worst of the war came today. Hair was pulled and flash tattoos gouged from skin during the soccer finals. Breasts slammed upon teeny breasts. At one point Hannah Biale threatened to tell everyone back home that Jordyn Luft can't shit unless she uses the camp director's bathroom. But the worst of it came at 1 o'clock, when the camp's supply of fireworks fired prematurely and sent both sides into a frenzy. For twenty-three minutes, it was as if the sky itself was ripping open. I took refuge at the lake upon which the boys' side lies. Rest assured, Mother, I shared no barracks with them, though I did commit to some hand stuff at Formal. Ultimately, once the hell-rockets cleared, ripped lanyards and downed fighters littered the grounds. Looking around the wreckage, one found herself thinking, these were real women. Not just soldiers. They had mothers; they had brothers and nannies and tutors and weekend tutors and maybe horses if they were blond.

So goes another day on the battlefield of Bryn Lake. Wish me luck tomorrow, dear Mother. You are my favorite cunt.

∽

Lance's carabiner finally gave out, and he fell, like, *bad* bad. We all saw his guts, so Color War's a tie. Coming home early. Let's book a teen tour for next summer.

Dr. Seuss Teaches Sex Ed

Did I ever tell you about the young dude
Who woke up hungover, and with a bad 'tude
Cuz he'd drank, and he'd drunk, and he'd drunk and he'd drank
So he went to the bathroom to unload his tank

Well, the dude stretched his arms, and his legs, and his chin
And he unzipped his pants, and he looked down within
And he saw what he saw, there's no doubt what he saw
What he saw there was more than a blip or a flaw

"But, oh, it's a bump!" the dude said with a shout.
So he sat down until he could figure it out
Yes this bumpedy-bump that appeared after boozing
Was making him think about past rendezvousing

So the dude took his 'tude, and his frattiest tank

And turned on his car with a screech and a splank

"To the doctor!" he said, feeling all of the scaries

As he tried not to cry—it would get on his Sperrys

When he got to the doc and they called out his name

The dude felt a new feeling—do they call it "shame"?

And the doc stripped him down, cupped his things with a tingle

And the dude held his breath as she looked at his dingle

"Sometimes," said the doc, "why, a spot's just a spot

Not a lump or a bump or a permanent clot

But some girls and some boys like each other a lot

So you better protect, and wrap up your mascot"

Oh, the things you can do with a dingle in tow

From blanking to blonking to getting a blow

"But alas," said the boy, "my long day seems to show

That you don't put your dingle in those you don't know!"

See You in Hell

Footsteps trample the forest floor. The crunch of dead leaves. The wheeze of ragged panting. A teenage girl—beautiful, terrified—glances frantically over her shoulder. She's running. But from who?

Her sneaker catches on a gnarled root. She stumbles, slamming into the earth. A man with butcher knives for hands looms behind her. She screams, crawling backward. The man's smile widens into a grotesque leer. He raises an arm and—*SLSHK!*—slashes through her chest. Her screams turn to gurgles. Her hands, flailing wildly, alight upon a fallen branch. As the knife-handed man rises, she summons all her strength, thinking of her bloodied friends back at the cabin, and she heaves the branch's jagged edge through his heart. The man crumples beside her. With her dying breaths, the girl turns to him and murmurs, "See you in Hell."

The next thing she knew, Kayleigh was in Hell.

She knew it was Hell because it was very hot and "Moves Like Jagger" was playing on a loop. As she got her bearings, she found herself standing in a long line of people. They were mostly old, all tapping a foot or drumming on their leg. Far in the distance lay a yawning pit of darkness and, nearby, a rusted sign like the kind you'd see at an amusement park. It read: WELCOME TO HELL. ESTIMATED WAIT TIME: 25,938 HOURS.

Kayleigh sighed, already inconvenienced by the afterlife.

"Jeez," groused a voice behind her. "This is gonna take a second."

The voice sounded oddly familiar. Kayleigh turned around, and—

"Stab-Hands?"

It was the man who had just murdered her moments earlier.

"Oh, he—heeey, Kayleigh." Stab-Hands shifted his weight from side to side. "What's—uh, long time!" He forced a laugh.

Kayleigh smiled back politely, eyes wandering in discomfort. She wasn't sure what to say in this situation. Namely the situation in which your killer and the terrorizer of the cabin where your best friends were slain on prom night shows up alongside you in the afterlife.

"Guess it makes sense, right?" Stab-Hands continued, rubbing his mangled jaw. "We died at—"

"The same time, yep." Kayleigh examined a cuticle.

"Yeah . . ." He hesitated. "You know, I'm sorry about . . ."

"Oh. Don't."

"Just—sorry, though."

"Me too." She turned around. "Well, ish."

"Right." He offered her a handshake. She took one of his blades gingerly and shook it. "'Ish' makes sense."

~

As the weeks went by, Kayleigh settled nicely into Hell. She liked her setup well enough: a small studio apartment surrounded on all sides by ferret-breeding neighbors. The neighborhood was okay, and after a while you got used to all the pharma execs. Not her favorite living situation, but she'd moved to Kips Bay after college, so she knew it could be worse.

Then one afternoon, Kayleigh found a note slipped under her door.

Lunch sometime?
—S. H.

Kayleigh pursed her lips. It wasn't like she didn't have the time.

"So how d'ya think you ended up here?" Stab-Hands asked, spearing a piece of wilted lettuce with his left knife.

"I don't know exactly," Kayleigh replied. "I never Venmoed my friends when they ran marathons, though, so probably that."

Stab-Hands nodded. "Oh, same here."

"Really?"

"*Oh* yeah. And if they called me on it I'd be like, 'Oh! I think I checked 'anonymous' by mistake.'"

"Exactly!" Kayleigh laughed.

"But no, I murdered scores of kids, so . . ."

"Probably it was that."

"Yeah, probably."

Kayleigh took a small bite of her meal. It wasn't great. In Hell, they mainly served fish dishes with foreign-sounding names so you couldn't even complain without sounding problematic. This one was called Cod alla Nicaragua, and Kayleigh was *not* about to go there.

"A little tough, huh?" Stab-Hands noticed Kayleigh struggling to cut her fish. "Here, I've got you." He reached over and sliced up the filet with ease.

"Oh, thanks."

"You should see me at hibachi," he said, twirling his hands.

Kayleigh chuckled. "You know," she found herself saying, "we should do this again sometime."

Turns out Hell is better with a buddy.

After a long hard day of coal-raking and genital-flaying, Kayleigh found herself, more often than not, meeting up with Stab-Hands to unwind. For a man who had devoted his life to dismembering horny teens, he was a pretty good hang. He was up on pop culture from research-stalking his victims, and though his vocal cords had been fried in the orphanage fire when he was five, he could bring it at karaoke night if he just lowered the key.

Whenever Kayleigh started missing home, she and Stab-Hands would spend the day by the infernal pools. He'd ask her about her classmates from the cabin—blond Jenny, Lucy the virgin, Matt the jock.

"Oh, Matt! I killed him right before you!" Stab-Hands once offered hopefully. "Maybe he's here somewhere?"

"Nah," Kayleigh said glumly. "He was the one who ran marathons."

Then one day, Stab-Hands didn't show up for improv class. (Hell had an eight-hour long-form workshop twice a week, obviously.) After about forty minutes of Zip Zap Zop, Kayleigh started to worry. "I'll be right back," she told her classmates.

"I'll be right back," they all echoed in Borat voices.

When Kayleigh arrived at Stab-Hands's apartment, his door was unlocked.

"Stab-Hands?" Kayleigh called out. She inched in carefully. He lived in a neighborhood with a lot of other murderers, and she wasn't trying to get stabbed to death twice. She heard a faint moan from the bedroom and dashed inside.

Stab-Hands lay facedown on the bed, his head in a pillow.

"What happened?!" Kayleigh asked. "What's wrong?"

He flipped over. She could see he'd been crying. "I'm sorry," he said. "I didn't want you to see me like this."

Kayleigh put a comforting hand on his blades. "What's going on? Tell me."

He took a deep, shuddering breath. "It's Braineater."

Kayleigh vaguely remembered the name from one of Stab-Hands's stories. "He was your friend, right? Or coworker?"

Stab-Hands nodded. "He died. Ran into the wrong orphan. They've been teaching them Krav Maga, because of all the—"

"Orphan-killing, yeah."

Stab-Hands blew his nose loudly into his duvet cover.

"But that's . . . a good thing, right?" Kayleigh knit her brows together. "Braineater will probably come down here!"

Stab-Hands flopped back onto his stomach. "That's the problem!" he groaned. "Braineater is, like, *the* guy. I'm going to be nobody compared to him."

"What?! Come on . . ."

"You have no idea how prolific he was, Kayleigh. He invented the—you know the thing where you close the medicine cabinet and the killer's behind you?"

"Yeah?"

"That was Braineater!" Stab-Hands exclaimed. "And all day I've just been thinking, like, what do I have to show for *my* life? A couple amusement park slaughters, a haunted dream, like, *once*." He shut his eyes. "Did I just waste the time I had?"

Kayleigh sighed. "Listen," she began, "you are the best murderer I know. Like, look at me! You murdered the shit out of me!"

Stab-Hands glanced at her. "You don't have to say that," he said drippily.

"I mean it! Remember how scared I was? Forget Braineater!

There's only one guy I want responsible for the death of me and my close friends!"

Stab-Hands forced a smile, but it faded just as fast. His mind was clearly still on his missed potential. His eternal mediocrity.

Kayleigh racked her brain for something to cheer him up. Then she had an idea. She sprang from the bed and twisted her face into a look of terror. "Oh, please," she said, starting to back away, "don't kill me! I didn't mean to touch that . . . that haunted amulet!"

Stab-Hands managed a weak smile. "I know what you're trying to do . . ."

Kayleigh picked up her pace. "If only we'd listened to the creepy convenience-store guy's warning!"

"Kayleigh . . ."

"Come on! Get up," she muttered.

Stab-Hands rose reluctantly. "You can't—like, escape or whatever," he offered.

Kayleigh jogged around the couch. "Oh no! Don't murder me! Not right before the big dance!"

Stab-Hands laughed and began to chase her. "I'm gonna make your insides your outsides."

"Oh no!" she yelled, waving her arms. Kayleigh pretended to trip over a table leg and went down. Stab-Hands dove to the ground next to her, laughing.

"Rah! Rah! Rah!" He mimed stabbing her.

"Noooo! Blegh," Kayleigh burbled next to him.

Stab-Hands smiled. He took a breath. "Thanks for that."

Kayleigh looked back at her friend. "Braineater who?"

Knock. Knock.

"Stabby Boyy!" Kayleigh swung open Stab-Hands's apartment door. "Get excited! I had to fight off *literal* Hitler for the last Four Loko—"

Kayleigh went silent at her friend's grave expression. Then Stab-Hands stepped aside to reveal a slender demon in a three-piece suit.

"Hi, Kayleigh." The demon adjusted his tie. "Come on in."

Kayleigh hesitated as she plopped down on the futon. "You know, now's not a great time . . ." she tried. "We were going to have a movie night, so—"

"This will only take a minute," he interrupted, gesturing for Stab-Hands to sit too. "Now, it's come to our attention that you two have been spending a lot of time together."

"Okay . . . ?"

"Specifically, it's come to our attention that you two are . . . having a *nice* time. And, you know, we can't have that. Because Hell and whatnot." Stab-Hands and Kayleigh exchanged a worried look. "So here's what we're gonna do . . ." The demon tossed a thick red folder down on the table. "Kayleigh, we took a look at your file, and honestly it's pretty mild stuff. Humming in public, falling asleep during *Moonlight* . . . Seems pretty marginal between here and, you know . . ." He whistled and pointed upward. "So to-morrow, we're gonna move you up to Heaven." He paused. "Yaaay."

Kayleigh jerked back. "But what about Stab-Hands?"

"Well, your pal Stab-Hands will stay here to really focus on what he's done. Sound good? Good." The demon stood up and eyed the Four Loko. "I'm gonna take this."

Kayleigh nodded numbly.

Then the door slammed shut.

"I'm not going."

Kayleigh and Stab-Hands had been sitting silently for what felt like an eternity. He looked up at her. "What do you mean 'not going'?"

"Literally that," she emphasized. "I'm not leaving you behind."

Stab-Hands shrugged. "You don't have a choice, Kay."

"Says who?" She sat up on the couch. "Like, what are they going to do? Put me in double-Hell?"

"Probably?"

"So we'll cross that bridge when we get there! We're a pack-age deal—"

"Kayleigh . . ."

"We can probably run this up the ladder, right? Hell must have a bureaucracy. That sounds Hell-y."

"Kayleigh."

"What?" She whipped around to look at Stab-Hands. His eyes had misted over.

"You need to go," Stab-Hands said softly. "You're better than me, Kayleigh."

"I'm not . . ."

"It's my fault you're even here. We can tiptoe around that all we want, but it's true. I doomed you to an eternity of improv and . . . foreign fish." He tenderly took her hand in his, and she softened at the feeling of the titanium. "You deserve more than this." Then he pulled Kayleigh into a hug. "You deserve more than me."

Kayleigh and Stab-Hands stayed up all night. Mostly talking, with some movie breaks and a rousing last round of karaoke. By the time the ball of screaming hellfire crested over the horizon, they were both snoring on the floor, the remnants of a hibachi dinner scattered around them.

Hummmmmm.

Kayleigh awoke to an ethereal chorus. She rolled over and looked at Stab-Hands.

"Want me to get that?" he asked. She nodded.

Stab-Hands stood up, opened the door, and ushered in two angels. They were beautiful, luminescent creatures, with white robes and halos that struck Kayleigh as a little much.

"Ready to go?" one angel asked.

Kayleigh turned to her friend, unable to speak for the lump in her throat. Stab-Hands enveloped her in one last hug. "She's ready." He smiled. "You guys got a good one."

And with that, Kayleigh left Hell.

"You're going to fit right in," one angel told Kayleigh as they rose into the sky.

"Your itinerary . . ." said the other, handing her a golden pamphlet. "Morning yoga at six, and then you'll do an hour of mindfulness before breakfast. Or, you know, just have an infinite orgasm in the belly of a star." But Kayleigh barely listened, her mind still on her friend back home.

One angel noticed. "You're thinking about him?" she asked. Kayleigh nodded. "Well, hey, your friend Matt's excited to see you! He's training for an ultramarathon. We've been hearing all about it." She put a hand on Kayleigh's shoulder. "You're going to love the rest of your eternity."

Kayleigh smiled. "You know what? I think you might be right."

Just then, they crested above the cloudline. A pearly palace towered before them. No lines. No sulfurous smell. Kayleigh took a breath of cinnamon-roll air.

"Enjoy," the angels said, floating off. "You deserve it."

Kayleigh took a peaceful moment. She soaked in this new place. This new life.

Then she reached into her sleeve and pulled out one of Stab-Hands's knives. A grin crept across her face.

If she stabbed fast enough, she'd be home in time for improv.

The Collected Works of Angsty Suburban White Kids Named Corey

Dartmouth

by Corey K.

Want to hear what I think of your phony-ass school?

Wait, really? Do I stand out in your applicant pool?

I meant to say, "I don't need school to succeed"

I'm a self-starter like the kind your campus might need

I meant to say, "Screw structure, I'm a teenaged Thoreau"

It says so on the résumé I pasted below

I'm active in my school and shit, but only to troll

Except for Spanish Honors Club, that place is my soul

Anguish, A Play

by Corey R.

Me: Good night.

Stepdad: Good night. I love you!

~

If It Weren't For

by Corey H.

If it weren't for

The unconditional support

Provided by my family, friends, and schoolteachers

As well as the categorical acceptance

I am afforded by my community

I swear to God I would kill myself.

But not literally.

~

The Stash

by Corey B.

I'd take a pill to soothe my blues
I'd Xanax through the evening news
I'd pop a Prozac, then some more
But Mom says don't go through her drawer

❧

XIII

by Corey S.

"On this sacred night, you'll grow," they said
Like a law of our theocracy
"You're a man now, son. You've grown," they said
Is that why I taste hypocrisy?

Like steely blood
Upon my tongue
Is that why I taste hypocrisy?

So without further ado, could all my camp friends please
come up to light Bar Mitzvah candle number eight?

⤳

Free Verse
by Corey G.

Meter and rhyme are for men

Who don't have enough acumen

Relying on gimmicks

They'll write up some limericks

And fuck no I did it again

⤳

Fab Four
by Corey Z.

Where did those four artists go?

We need Help since they've gone

In My Life they brought Revolution

And Yesterday, a song

A poem for Fall Out Boy

Who Am I?

by Corey M.

This mirror, mirror had no clue
The boy inside it hardly knew
My knickknack mind upon a shelf
I longed, I longed for sense of self

Who am I?
Who am I?

A frothy fire scorched inside
I cursed my mother, spat my pride
This question rang like bells pulsating
My steel-trap mind, reverberating

Who am I?
Who am I?

Then I met Carly Horner-Glass
A girl with band shirts in my class
I asked her out, she said, "Yeah, sure"
Dear aching corpse, I've found my cure

I'm Carly's boyfriend
I'm Carly's boyfriend

My soul now sings with purposed pitch
Said, "Sorry, Mom, you're not a bitch"
I got my self-worth after all
In a matching Styx shirt, extra-small

I'm Carly's boyfriend
I'm Carly's boyfriend

Carly and I laugh the same way
At fakers, fake love, child's play
When this Earth burns, you'll see the truth:
With Carly H. I'm fireproof

I'm Carly's boyfriend
I'm Carly. We are one

Now when we talk I can't distinguish
If it's me or Carly speaking English
But when we said, "I'm leaving you"
I knew it was her because I'd never say that

Who am I?
Who am I?

Rebecca Shaw & Ben Kronengold

Yikies!

This morning, police were dispatched to the Old Veranda Mansion in reference to a noise complaint. Upon arrival, police found two dismembered bodies belonging to the residents, as well as four colorfully dressed young adults self-described as "Junior Mystery Solvers." It became immediately clear to police that this group was unauthorized, as they, and this cannot be emphasized enough, kept looking for the "ghost who did this." Interviews with the group followed soon after.

Upon questioning, police learned that the Junior Mystery Solvers had solved cases before, but that their experience was limited to, quote, "spooky owls" and "mummies who turned out to be spooky owls." In other words, this was their first bodily mutilation. Group member Lola Finky was the first to find the bodies, reacting, quote, "Wowzers! So they're *dead* dead." This was followed by group leader Mikey Green volunteering to "taste the ectoplasm" off the corpses for "clues." He did not realize it was trace amounts of the killer's semen. "Salty!" Mikey exclaimed. "This must be a *beach* ghost!"

To make matters worse, team member Eugenia Newt found what she described as "the culprit's mask" in the study. She decided to put on the mask so as to "get into the bad guy's mindset." Unfortunately for her, the "mask" was actually the flayed face of yet a third victim, adhering to Eugenia's face by, as you might suspect, more semen.

Note: the Junior Mystery Solvers are all white, but you already knew that.

This investigation is ongoing.

FEBRUARY 12, 0800 HOURS

Last night, police were called to Barnaby Ranch in reference to suspicious activity. Upon arrival, police found the Junior Mystery Solvers again on the scene, quote, "riding the clue train" at yet another gruesome murder. Interviews began immediately once police ensured the group wasn't eating any cum off the crime scene.

According to reports, the team was, quote, "eager to help" and "ready to find this slimy, slimy ghost." Team member Grungy Clark then informed police that the ghost "wasn't in this suitcase of taco meat, dude," as he had "tasted it to make sure." Upon learning that the "taco meat" was actually the remains of a victim, the group exclaimed, "*Grungy . . . !*" in disappointed unison. This preceded Grungy's response of "Not againnn!" which was concerning to put it mildly.

For her part, Eugenia reportedly found a second victim while searching for clues in the farmhouse. Fortunately in this case, the victim was still alive and a first aid kit sat feet away. It was at that point, however, that Eugenia lost a contact lens on the floor and proceeded to search for it for over forty minutes. "Gee-yoinks," she was heard saying after the victim bled out. "It was in my eye this whole flangin' time!"

It should be noted that this time, the Junior Mystery Solvers brought with them their pet parrot, Click, who can only be described as "sickly" and "hoping to die." "End meee," Click was heard pleading, "end meee." Grungy informed Click that he was "hungry too, man" but that there was "no ectoplasm this time." He then nudged the parrot knowingly and said he could, quote, "get him some later." Grungy was promptly taken into police custody to find out what the hell that might mean.

This investigation remains white and ongoing.

FEBRUARY 27, 1200 HOURS

Early this morning, police were called to Moonlake Docks in response to several distress calls. To our surprise, the Junior Mystery Solvers were once again on the scene, prompting an internal review about how four kids in a van are getting to crime scenes faster than the police.

This time, however, the team's demeanor had notably shifted. Mikey told police that they, quote, "just hoped to observe this time." Eugenia added that they "may be out of their depth with this case" and "wanted to let the grown-ups lead." At this moment, it became clear to police that this was a group of kids with good intentions, ultimately driven by a desire to help others. Then Click coughed up a clump of human hair and interviews began posthaste.

"Soooo, we did bad," Lola confessed. "Mistakes were made, and we were the ones who made those mistakes." Police learned that the group had first arrived to find three injured victims floating at sea. To their credit, the team tossed out a life preserver and was prepared to rope the victims in. It was at that moment, however, that team leader Mikey suggested they "split up" and "search for clues," leaving the victims to drown just feet from the shore.

According to Lola, the group then spotted a "wild-eyed man" with a "bloody axe" trying to escape via kayak. The man was struggling to flee, however, as his tether was caught on the dock. Believing this man to be the killer, the group ran over and apprehended him. However, in a frankly stunning turn of events, the group then reminded themselves that "duh-doy, ghosts don't need boats," and proceeded to untangle the kayak and set the man free. In his parting words, the suspect mentioned he was "exhausted," at which point the team pointed his kayak toward a nearby children's hospital where they "might have an extra bed." It wasn't until they heard screams across shore that they realized they had made a mistake.

In a last saving grace, however, the killer's hat blew landward. Inside of it, several clumps of hair emerged as potential DNA evidence. This was, in no uncertain terms, a remarkable break in the case. Unfortunately, just moments before police arrived, the malnourished Click seized on the chance for sustenance and ate the human hair. Then minutes later, he flew into the blades of the police chopper to end his life. While no case of avian suicide has ever been reported, Click's final words were, notably, "I hope there's no soul. For the love of God, let there be darkness."

"*Cliiiick . . . !*" the group exclaimed in disappointed unison. "That one's our yikies."

This investigation remains ongoing.

college

Caesar's Relieved

Julius Caesar kneels, the Senate around him. Casca strikes with his dagger. The others rise up and stab Caesar.

CAESAR: Ohhhh shit! Well, shit. *I'm* relieved! I thought you guys were just hanging out without me. No, really! No, I'm serious! These past few weeks I've been like, *Is there a weird vibe? Like, are people excluding me from plans?* But this makes *much* more sense. You can't imagine the weight off my shoulders.

No, I mean it! It's all good! I was more just worried, like, did I say something wrong? Like, have I been talking about myself too much? But now I get that you were just plotting my death to cleanse tyranny from the Republic. I feel *at least* ten pounds lighter. Do I look ten pounds lighter? Don't count the blood loss. Haha!

Whew, man. Life. Friendship. *Guy groups*, am I right?! I'm talkin' *boys! Boys! Boys! Boys!* Imagine I was fist-bumping you guys during that. I would've fist-bumped each of you, but—the wounds.

Okay, stop. Stop, don't feel bad! This is, like, *way* better than the alternative. Do you guys know how gaslighted I was feeling? Really! Like when I asked what everyone's Ides plans were and no one answered? Now I know why! Or when I'd walk over while you guys were talking in the Senate and you'd just go, "So . . . *yeah.*" You weren't mad. You were just regiciding! Sorry for doubting you boys. Salads on me? Niçoise?! Nahh, just kidding. Casca got it!

Okay, I feel like I'm seeing some glances around the room. Guys. It's! All! Good! I'm just relieved because I introduced a lot of you, you know? I don't want to feel like, oh, I was friends with Metellus and Casca first and now they're plundering city-states without me. Or, oh, I introduced Decimus to Brutus and now they're boys, hitting the bathhouse together. And shit, speaking of Brutus. *Bruuutus.* You too, bud? Man, we have fun.

Whew. 'Cause, like, I'm still the leader, right? I feel like, well, not the *leader* anymore because—*Stab! Stab! Ahhh!* But, like, definitely the glue of the group, right? 'Cause I feel like you guys wouldn't have gotten close without me, ya know? I just feel like a lot of the side chats were kind of *about* me?

I guess? Does that sound right? I see a few nods. Casca nodded.

Anyway, this has been crazy. Classic boys' story that *all the guys* were there for. K? We were all there. Don't forget that part. And, uhhh, yeah! Just don't hang out when I'm gone! Am I right?

What do you mean "drinks after this"?

Fuck!

College Stories Fact Check

Some of the best memories we share together are from college. We were lucky to spend four years writing comedy, drinking heavily, and making some of our wildest memories during school. The only problem is, we were both there for all of it. We met at a Yale accepted students meet-up and started dating the first week of freshman year. Which means that for every epic and crazy college story, there's always someone there to remind us how it really happened. Some examples below:

BEN: I didn't take myself too seriously in college. During the first week of school, I got invited to a Pikachu Party off campus. A Pikachu Party! I spent the whole night living out my childhood nerddom, debating the best starter Pokémon, taking shots for every legendary Poké we could name on the spot . . . That's when I knew: I belonged at this weird, wonderful school, and I was going to find my people.

REBECCA: Ben misheard "Pikachu Party." He misheard it badly. Ten minutes in, an upperclassman stands on a table and screams, "You know what you're here for!" and sixty-plus college kids stripped bare-ass naked. It was a Peek-at-You Party. As in, everybody gets a "peek at you." Ben, the lone idiot in the Bulbasaur onesie, hid in the bathroom and had a full panic attack. He finally reemerged with his nipples poking out of said onesie and was politely asked to "show peen or leave, Bulbasaur." Needless to say, Bulbasaur left.

• • •

REBECCA: Friends on campus were easy to come by, and I lucked out almost instantly. I met my friend Sam in September of freshman year. We bonded over funny stories about our parents and have been best friends ever since. What can I say? It just came naturally to me.

BEN: Rebecca's first college friend was the campus rabbi. She attended so many Hillel events in her first week of school, people thought she was converting. Stumbling back from her fourth Rosh Hashanah mixer, Rebecca ran into a group of girls on the freshman quad. One girl named Sam started a story, "The funniest thing happened to me last week—" and Rebecca laughed so hard before the punchline it was like she malfunctioned. She salvaged the friendship months later and did, in fact, trade out Shmueli for Sam.

BEN: College is where I became a romantic. Dating Rebecca from the first week of school meant I had to constantly bust out surprises. So for our first Valentine's Day, I hired an a cappella group to march into her seminar and serenade her with a song. Rebecca knew, in that moment, that I was the one. Best. Gift. Ever.

REBECCA: It was a shitshow. He paid an a cappella group to come to my four-hundred-person LECTURE, interrupt a lesson on ABORTION ETHICS, and sing "My Funny Valentine" a foot away from my face. If you're not familiar with the lyrics, which Ben fucking wasn't, here are some of them:

> *Your looks are laughable*
> *Unphotographable*
>
> . . .
>
> *Is your figure less than Greek?*
> *Is your mouth a little weak?*
> *When you open it to speak*
> *Are you smart?*

Et-mother-fucking-cetera.

We didn't speak for two days, and I hired the same group to sing "My Funny Valentine" during Ben's final exam. For the next three years. Bitch.

• • •

REBECCA: My sophomore year I joined the Pi Phi sorority, and I have to say, I'm glad I did. Sure the parties were great. But my best memory? A charity event we held to raise money for female literacy. It was meaningful work for a great cause. I won't forget that night anytime soon.

BEN: Rebecca forgot that night immediately. She did somewhere between eight and forty-eight Jell-O shots and went around the event saying they were "raising money to teach the Pi Phi girls how to read." Then she disappeared for three hours, and I found her in a Chipotle bathroom looking like what can only be described as "Ozzy Osbourne's sewer ghost." The next day, she issued a formal apology to the sorority. And the Chipotle.

• • •

BEN: I bounced back from the Pikachu Party hard. By junior year, I was comfortable letting loose and trying new things. On the night of Spring Fling, the big campus music festival, we drove out to Lighthouse Point with our friends, and I thought, *Fuck it, let's skinny-dip.* I took off all my clothes, ran into the ocean, and thirty of our favorite people followed suit. It was a perfect memory.

REBECCA: There is no ocean at Lighthouse Point. It's a shallow, rocky inlet of the Long Island Sound that's a few inches deep at best. Ben ran in fully naked, and only then realized how shallow it was. Screaming, he lay on the ground and started splashing water onto his naked body, desperate for the mercy of submersion. All our friends watched in horror, and no one followed. Bulbasaur showed peen that night.

• • •

REBECCA: Jumping ahead to senior year. I'm not going to say I was in a secret society, but I'm not going to say I *wasn't.* If I was, though, let's just say this: the traditions were timeless, the rituals were sacred, and the secrets I learned will never, ever come out.

BEN: Rebecca was in Aurelian Society. It has a Wikipedia page; look it up. The traditions included getting drunk in a hotel room twice a week, throwing a Christmas party, and accidentally "leaking" the full list of its members to the campus gossip paper at the end of the year. Now I, on the other hand, was in a secret society, and the traditions were timeless, the rituals were sacred, and the secrets I learned there will never, ever come ou—

REBECCA: It was the same. They were all the same, and everyone was in one.

• • •

BEN: On our last day of college, we were fortunate enough to give a graduation speech in front of our classmates, our families, and guest speaker Hillary Clinton. On an earnest note, it was the most special day of our college careers, and we'll be forever grateful that a moment of oratory and comedic revelry was the platform for us to jump-start our professional lives.

REBECCA: We made a dick joke in front of Hillary, and we've been paid to write dick jokes ever since.

Butterscotch Galaxy
(Or, the Spectacular Class of 54)

This year at NYU, 9.2 percent of incoming first-year students missed the deadline to submit their housing form. Jeremy Hedder and Malik Niang were among that 9.2 percent.

For his part, Malik Niang was among the 3 percent of international students who forgot the midnight cutoff. He was from Senegal, so while he could technically blame the time difference, it would be more honest to blame the new season of *Attack on Titan*, his favorite anime to get high to.

Jeremy Hedder, on the other hand, was part of the smaller .04 percent who couldn't decide whether to come out on his online questionnaire, thus missing the deadline after three hours of debating whether he was regular gay or full "drop-down-menu gay."

So when Jeremy and Malik were matched up as roommates, there wasn't an obvious rationale. They didn't have academic overlap or a shared interest in sports. Malik was a morning person, while Jeremy's Adderall prescription kept him up late, usually crying at videos of soldiers coming home to their dogs. On their first night as roommates, Malik woke up at one a.m. to the sound of Jeremy sniffling. "What's the matter?" Malik asked. Jeremy angled his laptop out. In fifteen minutes' time, they were both on Adderall crying together.

The Senegal Appreciation Club at NYU is fairly new and rather Jewish. Specifically, Malik and this kid Amadou started it after orientation and made Jeremy join, so now it's technically one-third Jewish. While most first-years fluttered about the Club Fair, scouting activities and raiding Starburst bags, Malik and Jeremy worked a table. They handed out flyers for the Senegal Appreciation Club, answered questions about Senegalese culture, and quickly realized that some Senegalese things are not *actually* "Senegalese things" but are rather "everywhere things" (rice pudding, teen angst, the movie *Shrek 2* . . .).

By the end of the day, Malik and Jeremy were down forty flyers and one founding member, as Amadou got recruited by all seven sketch comedy groups. (He was funny, but more important, he *knew* funny.)

"This was a bust," Malik said to Jeremy as they dragged their trifold back to the dorm. "Should've just signed up for a real club."

Jeremy shrugged. "So we won't write for the school paper. Or do stupid rocketry," Jeremy said. "College isn't about all that extra shit anyway."

Malik smiled at him. "True. College isn't about all that extra shit."

~

But it turns out college is about all that extra shit. And just because two people say something doesn't mean it's true.

Over the next few weeks, the Club Fair misfire put Jeremy and Malik one solid step behind the rest of their classmates. On weekends, they didn't have a group chat telling them where to go or what to do. They only knew if a party was happening if they overheard it in a dining hall, and when they *did* successfully hunt down a party, there was usually a theme that left them starkly out of place. One time they just showed up as lobsters and simply hoped for the best.

By the time they figured out what frats there were, the pledge classes were already chosen. And by the time Malik discovered the Anime Society, their watch parties were full and he had to "rush again in the spring." The closest Jeremy got to an extra-curricular was joining the Consent Education Club as "Drunk Boy Who Gets Slapped" in their reenactments. After nine open-palm strikes to the face in four different middle schools, Jeremy decided to part ways with the group, only to get slapped again.

"Butterscotch Galaxy." Malik swung open the door to their dorm room.

"What?" Jeremy groaned, laying his smarted cheek on his pillow.

"*Butterscotch*," Malik emphasized, "Galaxy." Jeremy rolled over as Malik unfurled a small plastic bag. Inside of it, a lone pre-rolled joint.

"Where'd you get that?"

"You know that girl in my psych lecture? Broke her arm? I've been taking her notes?"

"Yeah?"

"This was her goodbye present."

"Oh, great! She's better?"

"Nah, dropped out. My notes were shit."

"Ah."

Malik lobbed over the baggie. Jeremy studied it. "So this is it?" Jeremy asked. "We're gonna be stoners in college?"

Malik shrugged. "Only one way to find out." Then, with all the confidence in the world, he clicked the button on a USB drive. "Oh is this not a lighter—?"

"That's not a lighter."

"Whoops."

There are three types of kids who use the student kitchen in college. 1) Liberal arts kids having a breakdown, supplanting therapy with something called "slutty brownies"; 2) Romantics trying to woo a date with kinky flour fights and salmonella; 3) Desperate first-years trying to find a lighter or, if that fails, a gas-burning stove. Jeremy and Malik were in the last category.

"Turn it—just push the knob and turn," Jeremy back-seat instructed.

"I did! Why's it clicking, though?!"

The gas burner provided a metronome for their joint incompetence. Until finally . . .

Whoosh.

"Theeere we go! See? You had to *push* and turn."

Malik gave Jeremy an appropriately burning look. Then he unbagged the joint, dipped it into the stove grate, and watched as a fiery tendril kissed the paper. *Crackle. Crackle. Sizz.*

Malik looked at Jeremy. "You first."

Jeremy brought the joint to his lips, pulled with not enough force, and then suddenly way too much force. "Oh no." Then Jeremy coughed. Then Jeremy coughed some more.

"Gimme some, gimme some." Malik took the joint and pulled, attempting Os, but producing what looked more like three 0s and one ° if you really looked closely.

"God," Jeremy managed. "What'd you say this stuff was called?"

"Weed."

Jeremy rolled his eyes. "No, the *type*," he coughed out.

"Oh. Butterscotch Galax—"

Then Jeremy and Malik went shooting through space and time.

The first thing to know about interdimensional travel is that it's not how it looks in the movies. You don't pass through endlessly colorful worlds. You don't jolt around a field of stars as your cheeks flap helplessly. Instead, it's dark. And you can hear infinite versions of yourself screaming. And if you do it with someone else, then you almost always meld minds and hear each other's thoughts for a moment.

Malik was thinking, *Shiiiiit.*

Jeremy was thinking, *Water.*

Pop!

Malik and Jeremy reemerged in a swirl of themselves. Their own matter and hair and untoned limbs spun around the air like floss sugar, eventually solidifying back into two gangly eighteen-year-olds.

"Dude, whoa . . ." Jeremy began. It felt like the right thing to say after a weed-induced time warp, if a bit on the nose.

They took in their surroundings. They were in a small room, not too different from the one they'd been plucked out of. But the sterilized Formica had been replaced by a wooden counter. Modern cabinets were suddenly unhinged and worn, and hundreds of green and clear bottles gleamed along the walls.

"What in the . . . ?"

"You putzes just gonna stand there?!"

Jeremy and Malik whipped around. A man in a cotton shirt, with big teeth like the kind they don't make anymore, was hoisting a Smirnoff box behind them. "Help a guy!"

"Oh! Sure."

The roommates hurried over, lifted from their knees, and settled the Smirnoff box in place.

"Sorry, sir—" Malik started.

"Just pay attention next time."

"No, I mean, sorry, but where *are* we?"

The man looked at him, then at Jeremy. Then he took an aggravated breath. "Christ. Lay off the blow, please. It's barely two a.m." The man pushed past them, exiting the musty liquor closet. "And would you take the fuckin' shirts off?!" he called over his shoulder. "This isn't the foo-foo Copacabana. This is Stu—!" But the man disappeared into a mess of lights and sound. Jeremy watched him go. Then he turned back to Malik, whose shirt was halfway over his ears.

"What are you doing?!" Jeremy asked.

"Do you really want to get yelled at by Calamity James?! Just do it!"

Jeremy rolled his eyes, pretending to get the reference but really just making a mental note to Google it later. Then he pulled his shirt over his head too.

"Where'd he just say we were, Jeremy?" Malik asked.

"I didn't hear him right," Jeremy said. "'Cause what I *did* hear made no fucking sense."

Then Jeremy crept toward the door, heart beating in his barely hairy chest. Until finally . . . he pushed it open.

"What the f—"

"Never mind. I heard him right."

For two kids who couldn't get into a frat or the Anime Society, Studio 54 at the height of the '70s was a dramatic change of pace. A Technicolor flurry lit their ashen faces. Pulsing stage lights that looked like they belonged on another planet enveloped people who looked like that planet's gods. Chic's "Le Freak" burst out of nuclear speakers; everyone knew all of the words and none of them. Also, there was a horse on the dance floor.

"Service!" A waiter barged toward them, offloading a tray of drinks to Jeremy, then another to Malik. "Group of three in the back. Go."

"Oh. We don't work . . ." But Jeremy was stopped by the sight of the waiter. He too was shirtless. His track shorts were just a hair shorter than the boxers Jeremy had been doom-napping in earlier, and subsequently traveled to this era wearing. Save a glossy coat of sweat, Jeremy and Malik were dead ringers for the waitstaff.

"I said, 'Service!'"

"Sorry! Got it!" Jeremy blurted. He and Malik took the precariously loaded trays and turned to the dance floor.

"What. The. Shit."

Traversing Studio 54 with a tray of cocktails takes Olympic-level skill, and Jeremy and Malik were not Olympic-level skillful. However, they *were* college students, so they approached the problem like any college students would: thoughtfully, analytically, and by doing three tequila shots each to lighten the load. Their list of early obstacles included a ballerina on roller skates, an eighty-two-year-old woman being wheelbarrowed by a nun, the wrong half of the Jackson Five, and finally, said horse.

"You good?!" Jeremy shouted over the music when they were finally out of hind-leg range.

"All good in the—*oof!*" Then Malik got nut-tapped by Fran Lebowitz and spilled his entire tray onto himself.

"Fran!" a breathy voice parted the crowd. "Sorry about her. Come here, dear, I'll clean you off." Malik staggered forward, pulled in by some sort of . . . *gravity*. And then suddenly, without even realizing it, he was being wiped off by legend of stage and screen Elizabeth Taylor. Also without realizing it, Elizabeth Taylor was wiping off the future former president of the Senegal Appreciation Club. Jeremy was aware of both of these facts, though he thought it best to stay quiet.

"Thanks, ma'am."

"Oh, don't call me 'ma'am.' 'Liz' or 'that drunk bitch' work just fine." Elizabeth patted Malik's shoulder. "But I prefer 'Liz.'"

"Well, thank you, Liz."

"You sit down. *You* . . ." Liz Taylor whipped to Jeremy. "Double the drinks and come back thirsty. We'll need help polishing them off."

"Oh," Jeremy began. "You know, I don't think that's a good idea—"

"One second!" Malik interrupted. Then he took Jeremy's arm and whisked him aside. "BRB, Liz. *Erm*—be right back."

"Huh! I like that," Elizabeth Taylor said to herself. "*B-R-B*."

"Dude, what are we doing?!" Jeremy asked.

"I know. This is crazy!" Malik said, eyes electric.

"No, I mean we have to get out of here."

"Okay, sure, sure! But first . . . *you* have to get us more drinks."

"No. No, no—" Jeremy shook his head.

"Dude! Yes! Do you know who these people are?!"

"Do you?!"

Malik paused. ". . . Not really, no. But still, how sick!"

Jeremy opened his mouth to argue. Malik jumped in.

"Look at me." He took Jeremy by the shoulders. "We are at the biggest party, in the biggest club, in the biggest fucking—*decade* in history. We are in. It's finally happening!"

Jeremy processed this. It *was* a sharp departure from what they had going for them back home. There was a new, exciting feeling that they were in the right place at the right (well . . .) time. But Jeremy shook off the thought.

"No, dude. Malik. We could be *stuck here*. We could be trapped here for years. We could get *Interstellar*-ed on our way back and meet our daughters when they're grandmas. We're—I don't know how to talk to old people!"

"We'll cross the grandma bridge when we get there!" Malik insisted. "Just one night. *One night* to be a part of something." He gave it one last push. "And we'll figure the rest out later."

Jeremy studied Malik's resolute eyes. He was certain. Then finally, Jeremy exhaled. "We'll figure the rest out later."

This time, two people said it. And this time, they were going to make sure it was true.

Malik smiled. "The anime club can get fucked."

The beautiful thing about Studio 54 was that everyone was part of the party. Or rather, everyone *inside* was part of the party. The crowd outside could go "jerk off to their mothers," as the manager thoughtfully reminded them throughout the night. But the insiders—the patrons and bartenders and bouncers and performers and waiters and animals—they all melded together like hot lava. Jeremy and Malik were just red-hot air bubbles bursting in the mix.

In their role as waiters, Jeremy and Malik took the treacherous Tray Walk eighteen more times that night. By the sixth time they were doing it separately. By the tenth time, they were incorporating a shot with a senator or a grind line with the Osmond siblings. At four-thirty a.m., Jeremy and Malik met back up, coated in feathers and alcohol sweat.

"Dude! I just took something called a 'speed balloon'?!" Malik blurted out. "Anyway, I'm a centaur now, and I have three fairies, which is the right amount!"

"That's awesome! And I just made out with a woman. A *woman!*"

"Wha—? Who?!"

"I dunno! She said her name was Ziggy Stardust!"

Malik's expression dropped. "Bro, even *I* know that one."

The entire night was a whirlwind of dancing and drugs and brushes with superstardom. But the real highlight of it all proved to be Liz. Liz Taylor checked in on the guys again and again throughout the night. And whenever she did, she'd whisper little tricks to navigate the club. "Pryor's in a tipping mood. Go over." Or, "If Truman Capote asks you questions, avoid. You'll end up a necrophiliac in his next novel." She was quickly becoming the cool older girl they had hoped to meet in their first months of college. The kind of big-sister type who probably would've turned things around for them, but who'd never materialized. Something about Liz was just comfortable. And comforting. So when things finally started to settle down for the night, Jeremy and Malik decided to pull Liz aside and tell her the truth.

"What's the matter?" Liz asked in an accent that would be described today as "Lindsay Lohan British."

"We wanted you to know that . . ." Jeremy swallowed. "Actually, can you . . . ?" He nudged Malik forward.

Malik took a breath. "We wanted to tell you that we're not actually from here."

Liz's violet eyes darted between them. "Okay . . ."

"Like, we're not supposed to be here," Malik explained. "We traveled from another time. Or another dimension, or something."

Liz paused. Then she laughed a little as she took them both by the hand. "Oh, boys," she said, leaning in close. "How do you think any of us got here?"

Jeremy and Malik's eyes widened. And with that, Liz glided

off. Then she tripped over a table full of cocaine and crashed through the glass. She was drunk. She was very high and drunk.

"$7.50 . . . $7.50 . . ." Behind the bar, the toothy manager divvied up cash among the waitstaff. Jeremy and Malik drifted over. "$7.50 for you . . ." He thrust some bills and quarters toward Malik.

"Actually . . ." Malik spoke up. "Can I just have those instead?" He nodded to a box of official Studio 54 T-shirts under the bar.

The manager just blinked. "You want *T-shirts* instead of your pay?"

"Yeah." Malik pulled Jeremy in with him. "We both do, actually."

"You realize we give you those *for free*, right?"

But Malik just shrugged.

"Oh-kay, then!" The manager rolled his eyes. "Complimentary T-shirts sold for $15. Now get the hell out of here."

Malik hugged the box, lifted it up, and hurried off. He looked like he had just gotten away with murder.

"What—dude!" Jeremy chased after him. "Why would—we could've meal-swiped for $15!"

"Bro. Where we're going . . ." Malik said. "We don't need meal swipes." Then he paused for effect. "It's from a Senegalese movie."

"That's not a Senegalese movie, it's an everywhere—" But Jeremy bit his tongue and decided to let Malik have this one. "Okay, Mal," Jeremy said. "I trust you."

The second thing to know about interdimensional travel is this: waking up from it feels like a splitting hangover. After their negotiation with the manager, Jeremy and Malik reentered the liquor closet and emerged back in the present in the student kitchen, heads pounding to the rhythm of "Get Down On It." They were sweatier now, shirtless, and, to Malik's delight, in possession of souvenirs.

"Did it . . . ?" Malik glanced down. The cardboard box of shirts sat against the kitchen counter. "Holy shit, it came with us."

"Who cares about the shirts?! Malik. We just broke *time*. I taught Andy Warhol about *Hot Ones*. That was . . . We're—!"

"We're gonna be rich." Malik turned to Jeremy. His lips curled into a smile. The same look in his eye as when he first pitched Jeremy the Senegal Appreciation Club. Or when he brought the joint into their dorm room. Or when he said they should stay at Studio 54. Malik had a new idea, and it started with old T-shirts.

If there was one lesson the guys took away from their night at Studio, it was the power of a crowd. And as Malik and Jeremy set up a janky stand in Washington Square Park the next day, they were determined to attract the same kind of buzz that surrounded the nightclub itself.

The pitch was simple: one-of-a-kind, vintage Studio 54 T-shirts for 150 bucks a pop. Of course, the term "one-of-a-kind" was debatable. The shirts *did* travel through time and space to get here, which is a one-of-a-kind-type thing to do. On the other hand, there were forty-one of them, and they were all identical. But "forty-one-of-a-kind" didn't look as good on a banner.

Luckily, the student body didn't split hairs. Word of the vintage shirts spread fast among the Tisch hipster scene. As Malik had hoped, Studio 54 was a fascinating enigma to culture heads and downtown wannabe types alike, and 150 bucks for a shirt was a reasonable request for people who shared Venmos with their parents.

"Is it ironic?" one kid asked over Malik's pumping playlist.

"No. It's authentic," Jeremy answered, instantly proud of the way that scanned.

"Yo, give me four for my suitemates," a freshman drowning in an XL shirt said. "They're gonna love this." Jeremy beamed and grabbed a bag.

By the end of the week, they had sold over three grand worth of shirts. It was meal swipe money for the year and then some. Even better yet, the stand was becoming something of a social hub. Undergrads came by to browse and ended up staying all afternoon, sharing music and shooting the shit and chatting about thrift culture. (Turns out thrift culture was mostly just lying and saying your clothes were thrifted.) But over time, talk of vintage clothes turned to "Where are you from?" turned to, eventually, asking about evening plans.

"When you guys sell out, you should meet up with us at Doc Holliday's," one upperclassman said. "Theme tonight is Under the Sea."

Jeremy stifled excitement. "Yeah, we'll have to see if we have anything to wear . . ." Then he mouthed to Malik: *LOBSTER. COSTUMES.*

I! KNOW! Malik mouthed back.

The funny thing was, the promise of Studio 54 had been just one night of partying in the past. But the ripple effects, Jeremy was starting to understand, could mean finding their place in the present.

"You have the best fucking ideas," Jeremy said to Malik once the upperclassmen were out of earshot.

"Dude," Malik replied. "*We* have the best ideas."

The months that followed were no different. It was as if the guys' night with Liz, and the Osmonds, and the roller-skating grandma had knocked something into place for them. They were walking around campus with a newfound confidence. Malik started speaking up in class, not in a particularly smart or additive way, but he made his lit professor laugh once, which is really the most you can achieve without doing the reading. Jeremy even started chatting with a junior he met by the T-shirt stand. They made plans to get drinks, not this week but the week after—the junior had a paper due Monday, and Jeremy said he had to volunteer as if to sound busy and righteous.

At night, they would go to Doc Holliday's or the Palladium or a random park hangout. And slowly but surely, they started to build their *own* kind of party gravity.

"Ayyy! There they are!"

"Yo, what can I get you to drink, Malik?"

"Dude, Jeremy, have you met Tara? You *have* to meet Tara. Tara!" Tara was always disappointing. But still, just a few months prior they would have *killed* to meet a Tara, and Jeremy was keenly aware of that.

"Malik! Quick question!" Jeremy hustled across a party at University Hall. "Derek invited us to a thing at his frat tomorrow. Apparently, two pledges realized they're allergic to their own vomit and he said we can have their spots? What do you think?"

Malik just laughed. "Dude, no way."

"Really? Why not?"

"Do you think Liza Minnelli gives a crap about frat guys?"

Jeremy tossed his head back, chuckling. "Uh, no? Probably?"

"Also, hey, this party peaked an hour ago. Want to head out?"

"Oh," Jeremy said, glancing around as Malik floated toward the door. "Sure. Okay."

Then a slurry voice called out for Jeremy. "You're LEAVING?! It was literally SO nice meeting you."

"Back at you, Tara!"

"Your vibe is a legend!" she said through a hiccup.

"K, thanks! You too!"

"You hear that?" Malik said, wrapping his arm around Jeremy. "Who needs frats? Your *vibe* is a *legend*."

Jeremy couldn't help but smile.

Jeremy's smile lasted until the next morning. He lay in bed, fighting against a grin that kept gaining ground on his face. He couldn't remember the last time he had felt this way—so uniquely himself, and yet so bound to a community. But here he was, feeling all of these things at once, waging war against a smile.

"We gotta do another drop!" Malik swung the door open. It was becoming a signature move of sorts.

Jeremy turned to him, brow furrowed. "What do you mean 'another drop'?"

"People are clamoring for more Studio 54 shit. We gotta sell more merch."

"But we don't *have* any more merch." Jeremy suddenly felt like a grizzled vendor at a Coldplay concert.

Then Malik hurried over to his desk. He lifted up a plastic baggie. There was still 98 percent of a joint left inside.

"No . . ." Jeremy saw where he was going with this. "Malik, no. Things are going great. What more could we want?"

"They're going great *now*. But we're only freshmen, dude! Don't you want all of college to feel like this?"

"Yes, but—" Jeremy took a breath. "I'm not risking it, dude. Sorry."

"Just one more time—!"

"I'm sorry."

In Jeremy's defense, he'd stick to his word. He wouldn't risk it one more time.

He risked it sixty-two more times.

The last thing to know about interdimensional travel is this: it's hard to predict where you'll end up. That night, Malik managed to convince Jeremy to come along for just one more visit to Studio 54. They smoked up, shot through the black void of space-time, and melded minds just like they did on the first trip.

Malik was thinking, *I'm doing this for us.*

Jeremy was thinking, *That's sweet, but I just shit my pants.*

The truth is, time-traveling is scary enough the first time you do it. But the first time it takes you to the *wrong place*? That's its own kind of unsettling.

"Is this right?" Malik asked, glancing around a dusty storage closet. "Are we back?" The smell of cigarettes and leather filled the air, mingling with the sounds of . . . was that *jazz*?

"Uh, Malik . . ." Jeremy shuddered as he stared at a whiskey barrel:

Malik hurried over. "Oh. Shiiii—"

THE CONSUMPTION OR DISTRIBUTION OF ALCOHOL IS A FEDERAL CRIME PUNISHABLE BY IMPRISONMENT

Jeremy swallowed. "I think we got too high."

"Hey!" Malik said. "We've got this. Let's just make the most of it."

Jeremy nodded, warding off an anxiety attack. "Yeah. Sure, we've got this."

They stepped into the 1920s speakeasy with the same playbook as they did at Studio: blend in, wait tables. Soon enough, they got their bearings, slinging moonshine and Charlestoning with the crowd. And by the end of the night, they were once again able to swap their pay in exchange for something of the time. This go-around, it was twelve bowler hats from the lost and found in exchange for their $1.25 pay.

"Bowler hats?" Jeremy asked.

"We'll find some soft boys in the philosophy department," Malik said. "They'll go rabid for this shit."

And they really, really did. When Jeremy and Malik returned to the present, the Washington Square Park stand yet again became the hottest spot on campus. They sold out of the hats in days. And suddenly, the blueprint was set.

The next week, they smoked a little less and landed in a cigar bar in the sixties. This time they got ties and handkerchiefs that were drunkenly left behind by admen. Four times after that, it was Max's Kansas City in 1977, at the birth of punk rock. They were too intimidated to ask for much, but they managed to sneak out with some guitar picks that they were able to pawn off on Steinhart kids for $12 a pop.

In reality, no matter when they ended up, Jeremy and Malik were able to make it work. Save for one disastrous trip to the Mesozoic era (scary) and one night in the 1830s when they got into a bar fight with John C. Calhoun, they were always able to turn a profit.

"I've been doing some reading," Malik would say around the dorm room. "If we end up in the eighteen nineties, we have to go for the overcoats. Those things looked fire."

"Nice. By the way, the mini-fridge we wanted was sold out, so I got two small ones to stack," Jeremy would reply. Suddenly, they had cash to go around, and their dorm was becoming the epitome of college luxe. That just meant it had a lot of phone chargers and a strobe light they used once. But still, it was more than they could've hoped for their freshman year. And most important, their place as the campus trendsetters, as the entrepreneurial it-kids who you *had* to meet, had been cemented in stone. Malik and Jeremy were in the *in* group.

"Best drop yet!" a friend would say.

"Think we can get another one this weekend?" another would ask.

"Eh, we'll probably take a break for a while—"

"For sure," Malik would correct Jeremy. "For *sure*, for sure."

By spring midterms, the night was finally upon them. "Well, last trip," Jeremy said, holding the tiny nub of the joint left in his fingers. "End of an era. Or *eras*, as it were."

Malik just nodded. "One second." Then he left the kitchen, biting his lip.

When Malik returned, he had a journal in his hand—one of those nice Moleskine ones, which he'd bought with their profits.

"*Buh, buh, buh* . . ." Malik placed the journal down on the table, rifling through the pages.

"Have you been . . . taking notes?" Jeremy read upside down. "What is this, your psych lecture?"

"So I think if we take half a puff—*no*." Malik's finger landed on a page. "If we take a *quarter* puff, and don't hold it in for too long, we can get back there."

Jeremy's brows knit. "Get back *where*?"

"Studio 54. For our last trip." Malik looked up, his eyes meeting Jeremy's. Almost desperate with hope.

"Okay . . . why there?" Jeremy was confused. After all these months, after all the places they traveled to, Malik still wanted to revisit *that* moment in time?

"It'd just be full circle. I was thinking," Malik said.

"Huh. I mean, I guess if you think you can get us there—"

But Malik had stopped listening. He just pushed—and turned—the stove knob.

Click. Click. Whoosh.

Jeremy and Malik emerged, for one last time, in a swirl of themselves. And to their shock, the sound of "Le Freak" emerged with them, blasting with a familiar, crunchy quality.

"No way . . ." Malik uttered as he glanced around a musty liquor closet.

"Well, well. If it isn't my favorite travelers," a silky voice said. The guys whipped around—and they met a pair of violet eyes.

Their final night at Studio 54 was even bigger and gaudier than their first. In the months since they'd last visited, the club had added a fog machine, flaming shots, and a bridge over the dance floor where Diana Ross performed a song that the guys tried Shazaming. Also, Jackie Kennedy was in town and was lowered from the ceiling not once, not twice, but five times. By the last time it was sort of like, *Yup, there she is. That's . . . still Jackie.* But still, it was all scope and spectacle and grandeur. It was all *Studio.*

"Okay, again? You were right." Jeremy turned to Malik. "Best night ever."

And Malik just smiled. "*We* were right."

By the time Diana Ross sang her reprise. Jeremy and Malik were swaying together, weeping on the dance floor.

"You bummed to leave?" Jeremy asked.

Malik looked over. An air of sadness to him. But also—a knowing look. Only Jeremy had no idea what he was supposed to know.

"What?" Jeremy pulled away. "*What?*"

"I'm not leaving."

Jeremy jerked back. "Funny."

But Malik just shrugged. "I'm not kidding. I'm staying here, man."

Jeremy tried to process. "You can't—how would you even do that?"

"We always walk through the liquor closet to get home, right? So I'm just . . . *not* gonna walk through."

Jeremy's mouth went dry. He shook his head.

"Yeah. I've been thinking about it for months. I'm pretty sure it'll work—"

"You've been *thinking about it for months*?" Jeremy shot back, catching Malik off guard. "All these trips. All this time together and you're *staying*. What are you—why?!"

But Malik didn't answer. He just traced his eyes across the dance floor . . . and landed on a sequined silhouette.

Jeremy followed his glance. "No . . . For her?!"

Malik's gaze locked on Liz. "She's really, *really* special, dude."

"Yeah, I know she's special. She's Elizabeth fucking Taylor! Everyone thinks she's special, Malik!"

"Well, we decided tonight that we didn't want to be apart again," Malik said.

"What—you *decided*?! Oh my God. Malik, do you hear yourself right now?"

But Malik *did* hear himself. He gave Jeremy a misty smile. "Hey, I really am gonna miss you, dude—"

"No, you won't!" Jeremy snapped back. "You're gonna miss dragging me through time. And me agreeing to all of your shitty plans. But I guess the plan all along was just to leave me behind?!"

"Dude, I'm not . . ." Malik threw his head back. "I mean, c'mon. You never thought we would meet other people? You never thought we'd find our partners? Grow our circles?"

"We *have* our circle. We're growing it together!"

Malik shrugged, at a loss. "We're just random roommates, Jeremy. Placed together for no reason. How often does that last—" But Malik stopped himself, as Jeremy's eyes went cold. "I'm—you know I don't mean it like that."

But it was too late. Jeremy felt like he was looking at a stranger. "No, you're right." Then Jeremy took off. "There was no real reason for us to be friends."

"Watch out for the—"

"Yeah, I *see* the horse!" Jeremy shouted back. He hadn't. But he wasn't about to let some random roommate know that.

The *actual* last thing to know about interdimensional travel is this: You need to be careful what you're thinking. Because in those quiet moments, when you're shooting through the screaming black void of space-time, when your mind is melding with the person next to you . . . you might just get your heart broken.

Every time they'd time-traveled together this past year, Jeremy thought something different. Usually *Ahhh!* or *Fuck, my stomach*, or *Can you mix Adderall and Dramamine?* But the last five *dozen* or so journeys they took together, Malik had the same thought. Every. Single. Time.

I'm doing this for us.

Jeremy sat at a high-top in the back of Studio 54 as he played these words over and over in his head. He had heard Malik thinking them time and again. And when Jeremy wanted to cut loose, or pump the brakes, or enjoy the real, *actual* present they had built for themselves, those words had kept him going. *I'm doing this for us.* This guy—this electric-eyed, possibly crazy, scheme-hatching friend—was doing this for *their* future. Except he wasn't. He was doing it for hers.

What pained Jeremy most was that he had the story all wrong. Not even the story. He had the *genre* wrong. This wasn't a tale of two friends journeying through time together, an unlikely, reality-bending friendship. This was a love story. Between two people separated by history. And Jeremy was just the random-roommate supporting character.

"Hey." Malik walked over.

Jeremy turned on his stool. He couldn't look Malik in the eye.

"I just—one thing, really quick." Malik reached into his pocket and took out his phone. Several clubgoers whipped toward them, jaws dropping at the screen.

"Dude, don't. You're freaking people out—"

"'I want a roommate with a sense of humor.'"

Jeremy stopped, eyes squinting. "What?"

"'I want a roommate who's up for an adventure, but always more excited about the people than the place.'"

"What is that—?"

"'A roommate with a sense of wonder. Who doesn't get jaded, because I sometimes struggle with that myself.'"

Jeremy shook his head. "You told me you missed the housing form deadline."

"I did." Malik shrugged. "I still wrote it. Just never sent it in."

Jeremy's breath shallowed, as Malik looked back down at his phone.

"'I want a roommate I can grow with. Hang with. Stay up late and cry with . . .'"

Jeremy listened.

"'. . . such that, no matter where college takes us, no matter where we end up in a decade's time . . .'" Malik looked up at his friend. "'We'll have always had that time together.'"

Jeremy's breath tightened as Malik put his phone away.

"You weren't random, man," Malik said to him. "You were exactly what I asked for."

Malik punched Jeremy's arm gently. Jeremy punched him back. Then they wrapped each other up in a hug.

"You were a great freshman-year roommate, Jeremy."

"*You* were a great freshman-year roommate," Jeremy answered. "And you're gonna be a great boyfriend."

Malik lit up. "Actually . . ." He lifted his hand. A wedding ring on his finger.

"Seriously?"

"Andy Warhol's ordained, so we just . . ."

"And so it begins! I miss the wedding invite!"

Malik laughed, then pulled a stool over and sat down.

The party raged around them for the next several hours. But the two friends just talked . . . and talked . . . and said their goodbyes. Maybe they'd meet again, some other time.

The next year at NYU, 7.8 percent of incoming sophomores missed the deadline for class registration. Jeremy Hedder and Malik Niang were among that 7.8 percent.

For his part, Malik Niang was living in the year 1979, getting rich on his groundbreaking Walkman "invention" and enjoying life as the fifth—and longest-lasting—husband to film star Elizabeth Taylor.

Jeremy Hedder, on the other hand, blew past the deadline for other reasons. He was out late with a group of friends, trying to convince Tara that she shouldn't get a tattoo. And by the time Jeremy got home, the deadline was minutes away. Could he have made it? Possibly. But instead he just stayed up late, on Adderall, watching old YouTube videos of a certain nightclub . . . cheering through misted eyes, as an old friend made out with three Osmond siblings at once.

He was doing it for them.

I Am Outraged

Me? I am outraged. I'm outraged by the issues affecting our country today. We've watched time and again as those in power wage war on decency. As a young citizen of this nation, I will speak truth to power against those who do wrong, and I will not rest, unless something more pressing comes up in my personal life.

Right now, this country needs a warrior. We need someone to pave the way and lead the movement. To stay vigilant and hold us to a higher standard. I'm willing to be that warrior until my ex calls about getting back together, at which point I'll need to take a break from warrior stuff to say "definitely yes" to that.

Because news flash: the "news" is getting it wrong. Every day, reporters say, "Let's talk about the issues." But I say, "Let's talk about the *power structures*." Let's talk about the systemic hierarchies that precede the issues until I hear that someone I know got pregnant, and then let's talk about that, exclusively, for three hours or more. Because who gives a shit about the power structure thing when we can get to the bottom of who knocked up Ashley?

So wake up, America! Because it's time to take action. The other week, I volunteered to drive a bus full of activists to a voting rights rally. I got in the driver's seat, turned on the engine, and then turned off the engine because seasonal depression strikes when you least expect it. Voting rights had to wait while I watched hedgehog videos in the lobby of a Best Western.

Because self-care can take precedence over political issues. Okay?! But there are still some threats to society that can never be ignored. For instance, I think about the blatant hatefulness of the alt-right all day long without exception. Period. Backspace. Except if I see something even vaguely sexual. Because if I do, I won't only not care about the hatefulness of the alt-right, I'll also forget what the alt-right is. "A music genre?" I'll guess haphazardly, like I just did.

I didn't vote because I thought my haircut looked weird that day. God, that feels good to get off my chest.

So friends, in this political age, I pledge to you this: I will arrive first to the march and leave last from the rally. I won't just sign the petition, I'll start the campaign. I will open my home to the disenfranchised and disregarded and yes, all of this depends on how secure I am with my social life and how happy I am with my weight.

So get out there, get active, and go on without me. The sun's about to set, and this warrior's feeling gloomy.

post-grad

How to Assemble Your First Couch, You Big Fucking Loser

You did it! You said a tearful goodbye to your college friends, handed your diploma off to Mom, and moved into your first-ever adult apartment. Now that the moving vans have cleared, it's time to face your first real-world challenge. A six-by-five-foot cardboard box looms in the corner of your empty living room. And you? Well, you're coming to terms with an essential truth:

It's time to assemble your first couch, you big fucking loser.

Step one is to take a long, hard look at your fucking self. Who do you think you are, ordering an assembly-required sofa like some Bob the Builder fuck? You think you have what it takes to put this shit together? You?? The kid who forgot to buy towels and has been *drying themselves off with a suitcase*?

And now here you go, sitting on your floor, looking up "how make couch" on your phone like the Patron Saint of Incompetence you are. You thought you were fucking cute doing this all by yourself? Waving your parents off with a "Thanks, but I've got it from here!" You probably pictured yourself whimsically hammering in screws in a pair of paint-smeared overalls, but you don't own any of those things, you fucking invertebrate. You don't even know where one buys those things, you Lexapro-filled cumsquash. You know so little that you missed the fact that you don't *hammer in* screws, you leaky fucking nipple. So much for your big adult moment, *Logan*. Oh, that's not your name? Well it is now, fuckwad.

All right. Heeere we go. Start unpacking those California Casual pillows from the box. Though let's be honest, there's nothing casual about you, is there? You planned your last six "random" hookups weeks in advance. You've already stained the cushions with your panic-sweat, and your next-door neighbor just texted you to **"keep it down with the crying."** Good fucking job, you waste of a microwaved pizza.

But oh nooo. The instructions say you need a screwdriver. "Why wouldn't they just include one?!" Here's why. Because they assumed you were a functioning adult, not an overgrown pimple who took over a host body. But hey, go for it! Stick a fingernail in there and try to twist it in yourself! You're not the dumbest person on the fucking planet, you're *resourceful*. Wink.

Oh man, turning to YouTube already? Guess it's not the worst place to find assembly instructions. But wait, you stumbled upon a vlog called "Kaitlynne and Keith Buy Their First House" and now you're doing a deep dive. Oh God, no. Noooo no. They're younger than you?! Next thing you know, you're lying facedown after learning Kaitlynne and Keith are twenty with two kids and a thriving business. Here's a tip: slide into

Kaitlynne's DMs, buy a subscription to Keith's protein powders, and realize you still haven't made any progress on your couch, you feckless amoeba fuck.

"He—hey guuuys?" That's you. That's an impression of you calling your parents back in Evanston, *Logan*. "Hey guuuys, can you help me assemble my couch?" To your surprise, your parents think it's sweet that you need a hand. They walk you through each step over FaceTime, and, after a couple of hours, the couch starts to slowly come together. "Tomorrow we'll add the legs!" they say as they blow you a kiss goodbye. You hang up, a smile on your face. Why? Because you're not alone. You're not a big fucking loser. You're a grown fucking adult who can ask for help.

"How'd we raise such a micro-shit?!" Dad says to Mom.

"Total fucking invertebrate," Mom agrees.

But you're never the wiser. Because now you're an invertebrate with a fucking couch.

My College Friend the Pope

It is a truth universally acknowledged that a woman in possession of a shitty job will spend Friday night drunk, semi-ironically watching *Ink Master* with a close friend. Tonight was no exception, and at approximately nine p.m. I was opening the door for Lauren, my college-roommate-turned-best-friend-turned-witness-to-the-time-I-drunkenly-DMed-Dave-Navarro-my-feet-pics. We settled in, toasting to finally having outgrown the boxed stuff, and began debriefing the week.

"So how's your—what'd you call it?"

"Oh, my reverse-finance internship?" I answered. "Not great. Yeah, turns out it means I pay *them*."

"Oof. So you quit?" Lauren grimaced.

"Not yet." I mumbled into my glass. "I feel like my boss likes me, so . . ." I took a deep pull of wine and changed the subject. "Mm! Did you read the piece I've been working on? No rush, but if you hated it just tell me and I'll disembowel myself."

"Oh yeah, loved it," Lauren said vacantly, eyes fixed on the screen as the judges tore into some schmuck's line work.

"Huh. The piece on Acadia . . . ?" I nudged her. "I'm thinking of submitting it to *Travel + Leisure*, so . . ."

Lauren snapped to attention. "Okay, *so* sorry. I didn't read it yet, but there's actually a good reason why."

"Oh! No worries. It probably won't get in anywa—"

"I've just been crazy busy with something really exciting and . . . *Whew*. Here it is."

"Is everything okay . . . ?"

"Literally perfect. Ahem. So you know how the Pope died last month?"

"The Pope—? Oh. Yeah. Sooo sad," I lied, cursing myself for scrubbing through *The Daily* for the cute commercials.

"And you know how I've been feeling pretty bummed out since I realized PR was basically just talking on the phone?"

"Of course. Yeah."

"Well . . ." Lauren's lips curled into a smile. "The College of Cardinals just met in Rome, and . . ." She pointed to herself and let out a squeal.

"What?"

"They chose *me*."

I just blinked.

"*I'm* the new Pope."

"You're the . . . new—?"

"Pope! I know! Can you believe it?!"

In all honesty, I couldn't. I mean, sure Lauren gave great advice, and she *did* have a perfect head for hats, but, "The Pope? You?"

"That's what I said at first!" she screeched, kicking her feet against the couch. "But honestly, Zo? Zo," she said, grabbing my arm, "I'm trying not to overthink it, you know? This is a huge opportunity for me, but we're all doing, like, *so* well in our careers post-grad. At our own pace, you know?"

I sat there, stunned. The buzz of the tattoo guns faded into a hum as Lauren beamed at me expectantly. All I could manage to say back was—

"Well, cheers, girlie!!"

And the rest of the night passed by in a blur.

Don't get me wrong. I was happy that my closest friend became a head of a theocratic state at age twenty-four. But I'd be lying if I said it didn't give me an occasional pang of inadequacy. Lauren and I had always been on pace with each other—I'd taken a so-so internship while pursuing travel writing; she had a PR job while trying to get her eco-friendly candles off the ground. We were both trying to do the thing we loved while doing something we hated. Then suddenly, she'd shot ahead of me. And I knew our careers weren't a competition, of course, but I also knew that if they were, Lauren's papal supremacy probably took the cake.

It wasn't long after our hangout that Lauren updated her LinkedIn status to "Future Pope" and Instagrammed a picture of rosary beads. I spent the rest of the day fielding texts from college friends. "So fucking pumped for her!!" wrote a guy saved in my phone as "Douchey Ryan."

"Ik. She's going to be great," I wrote back.

"She spent the semester in Italy, right?" another friend wrote.

"Actually, that was me," I replied, vaguely aware my jaw was clenching. "I got a grant to write about . . ." Fuck it. I deleted the message.

To her credit, Lauren kept our standing Friday plans. She still insisted that we start with how my week went, but intern happy hours suddenly felt trivial compared to robe fittings and cardinal politics.

"Cardinal Dolan is just, like, random. I feel like you'd love him, Zo. Oo, maybe I'll set you up!"

I gave Lauren a blank stare, waiting for her to get there.

"What am I thinking?" She slapped her forehead. "He's for sure gay."

As the weeks went on, Lauren's papal inauguration became all anyone could talk about. I was being asked about Lauren at parties, and anticipating Lauren's next *TIME* profile, and trying to remember why I'd thought Lauren was Jewish? Was I making that up? Then, before I knew it, I was boarding a flight to the Vatican for Lauren's big day. I squeezed into a middle seat, bracing for the fourteen-hour trek with a layover in Gdańsk. Lauren's childhood friends were flying direct, but my budget was tight, especially after buying the gold FROM NOPE TO POPE tank that Lauren's sister made us all order. "I mean, it's not like she's having a bachelorette party now," she texted us, linking to a pair of optional A BITCH'S PLACE IS IN THE VATICAN booty shorts.

When the ceremony finally began, it was pretty much what you'd expect: three hours long at the ass crack of dawn, watching bishops kneel before a girl I'd once seen clean Del Taco out of her hair. I landed in an empty seat next to Lauren's parents.

"Feels like yesterday you two were moving into your dorm room!" laughed her mom. "Now look at our girl! She looks so grown-up in her little outfit!"

"How's work for you, Zoe?" asked Lauren's father, filming the ceremony on his iPad. "Lauren says you're an internist?"

"An intern," I corrected him. "Well, reverse intern. I'm trying to do some writing, actually. But right now I'm at a really cool luggage start-up with a culture of internal promotion so . . ."

"Honey, look! Malala!" her dad called out, watching Lauren hug the Nobel laureate.

I took a breath. "Man. Lauren's home friends must be *so* jealous watching this. Like, what are *they* doing with their lives?"

"Well, Jamie actually *is* an internist, so . . ." Lauren's dad's eyes didn't leave Malala.

"Great," I said to myself. "That's great for Jamie."

When the ceremony ended, I finally got to speak to Her Holiness herself. Lauren's parents hosted a brunch at the Vatican for close friends and family. When I finally reached the front of the line, I wasn't sure whether to hug Lauren or kiss her ring, so I just settled on an awkward fist slap. "Proud of you, babe! When you rode that papal staff like a pony?"

"Sooo funny, right?" Lauren laughed, miming the giddy-up all over again.

"Ugh, I'm gonna miss our Friday hangs, though!" I sighed.

"About that . . ." Lauren began, a glint in her eye. She ushered me over to the side with her fifth-century ferula. "I actually have a surprise for you."

"Okay . . ."

She cleared her throat. "Zoe. How would *you* like to stay with me *here*?"

I was stunned. "What?"

"Before you answer, we don't have to pay maintenance—I already asked. And they said they'd push two beds together for you to make, like, basically a queen." My mind was racing. "Pleeease? We'd have the best tiiiime."

"But my job. You know, they really need me—"

"I already called them!"

"Oh?"

"They said they don't!"

I paused. ". . . Oh."

I took a long sip of my Communion wine. Then Lauren leaned in close. She lowered her voice. "Zo, please? We both know I'm in over my head here. Like, what the fuck is 'extreme unction,' anyway?" Lauren looked at me pleadingly. "C'mon. You can do your travel writing! You can write about Rome, and Vatican City, and we can keep our Fridays going! What do you say?" She beamed.

Then, with five simple words, I upended my entire life: "Well, ring-a-dang-dang, Miss Pope Thang!" I could've chosen better words.

I FaceTimed my parents that night with the update. They couldn't believe I was moving to the Vatican. I'd spent most of my life calling organized religion "the enemy of free thought," and more pressingly, I found pasta heavy. But they admitted that it was a great opportunity to ramp up my travel writing, and a much better vacation plan than visiting Aunt Rita in Denver. So with that, my journey began. Then it quickly ran into connection issues.

It turns out the Wi-Fi in the Vatican is questionable at best. And when I contacted the IT department to explain that I needed internet for research, they told me to "pray it stronger" and hung up. This meant that my writing would have to wait. Instead, I spent most of my first week following Lauren around. I sat at Mass and listened to her sermons and speeches. And honestly? I was proud of how well she was doing. Lauren actually had a lot to say on the meaning of virtue in a changing world, and she said "y'know" way less than she had during sorority rush.

But afterward, it was always hard to catch Lauren's attention. I kept getting swept up in the throng of pilgrims hoping to get their ailments cured. At best Lauren would pass me in the crowd, clutch one of my boobs like it was a baby, and go "Bless this tit!"

It made me feel special at first, but then I wondered if I was even in on the joke.

The only times I really got to see Lauren—*my* Lauren—were our Friday-night hangouts. However busy she was, however many orphans she'd deloused that day, on Friday at nine she'd knock on my door, wine goblets in hand. It felt great. We'd talk shit about the bishops and watch *God's Favorite Diners* on CatholicTV. But over time, it felt like Lauren's job was changing her. When I vented about the Wi-Fi, she assured me that "Saint Paul wrote with less, girl" and then did a little hand flourish that I could swear was just the Wu-Tang symbol. When I eventually picked up work as a restaurant hostess and complained about my boss, Lauren played devil's advocate. "He's probably just overworked," she'd say. Or, "Management is much harder than it looks. Have you tried asking for more responsibility?"

Another Friday, Lauren just rushed in, handed me a bag of vibrators, and hissed, "The nuns are coming. Guard these with your life," before dashing back out the door. Then she texted me, **"ok, nuns after our vibrators? how college is this lolol."**

Then soon enough, Lauren stopped showing up altogether. I let it slide once, assuming work got too hectic. Then it happened again, then a third time. By the fourth time I gave in and texted, **"We on for tonight?"**

"Yesss," she responded. **"I need this SO MUCH, dude."** It made me smile more than I cared to admit.

But a few hours later, I was still watching the clock tick by. Nine-fifteen, nine-thirty. Nine-forty-five. I called her. She picked up, frazzled.

"What's up?"

"Are you coming by tonight, or . . . ?"

"Ah, shit, I'm sorry. I had to grab dinner with this—some girl from work."

"Oh."

I heard a tiny English voice laughing in the background.

"Some girl?"

"Yeah, some—*old bitch*," Lauren laughed, playing to her crowd. The tiny English voice cracked up. "Some corgi-loving *biotch*," Lauren said. They were clearly a few drinks in. "But we're wrapping up. Should be done in fifteen."

But she wasn't. Midnight came around and I sat staring at untouched cartons of pad thai. Finally, Lauren showed up, flushed and giggly. "Sooo sorry. I couldn't get away. Ya know, royalty."

"*And* you're drunk. Great," I said.

"The queen is actually *so* fun, Zo. You would not believe— have you ever played croquet high?"

"No?"

"It's, like, her whole thing. She was telling everyone about it."

I bit my lip hard. "Who's 'everyone,' Lauren?"

She realized her mistake. "I'm—I'm sorry. It's like, I was stuck, though! What am I going to do?"

"Uh, invite me so I could be there?"

"I didn't think you'd want to come!"

"Why wouldn't I want to come? Because I'm not some pretentious head of state?!"

Lauren jolted back. "What's that supposed to mean?"

All the blood left my face. "It means that you take me for granted, Lauren. I found the one Thai place that delivers to the Vatican. The delivery driver got stopped at the border for *wearing shorts*. I walked all the way across the city-state to pick up food for us, and you couldn't even pick up your phone to text?"

"I'm sorry. Why don't you charge it to the Papal Mint and I'll—"

"It's not about the *money*, Lauren!"

"Look," she said, crossing her arms, tripping over herself briefly. "I'm sorry I have an important *job*, Zoe. I'm sorry people rely on me. I can't just call in sick, or drop something because I want to hang out with my BFF. Or, like, move across the world without anyone caring that I'm gone."

My heart dropped. "Get out."

"I'm sorry, that was too far—"

"NOW! Get out!"

Her Holiness collected her clutch and stumbled toward the door.

"You think you're so fucking special, Lauren," I said. "Don't forget, I know who you are. Three months ago you thought Jude Law was an archbishop, so don't act so fucking holier-than-thou."

"Actually, I *am*—"

"Yeah, I fucking HEARD it!" I shouted, slamming the door.

I didn't hear from Lauren for days. Not via text, or call, or smoke signal she'd occasionally send out to tell me to come streaking in the Sistine Chapel. Then one day I was trudging back from work when I heard her voice coming from my bedroom suite. The saddest part was, I felt kind of starstruck. This was my best friend, my *person*, but knowing she, in all her eminence, had come down to my quarters to apologize to me? I hated how important it made me feel.

Then I heard more voices. A cluster of sharp whispers, building in harshness as I got closer. I couldn't make out the words, but the tone was unmistakable: they were angry. I crept into my suite and peeked through the crack in the door. There was Lauren. With four red-faced nuns. And in Lauren's hand, the bag of vibrators she'd given me to stash. She pointed at them, a look of surprise on her face. And among the whispers, I could hear Lauren's voice saying one name over and over. "Zoe . . . Zoe . . . Zoe."

Lesson number one of living in the Vatican? Don't cross the Pope. That Holy Bitch will throw you under the bus.

I didn't wait to be formally evicted from the palace. I just hid out in the bathroom until the nuns left, then packed my things, and showed myself out through the stupid-big bronze door.

"Next in line!"

I shuffled to the front of the TSA checkpoint and dropped

my suitcase onto the conveyor belt. I held my breath as it chugged through the X-ray machine, wondering if the agents could see the little cross-shaped soaps I'd stolen from the bathroom on my way out. Once my suitcase was through, I looked out the window one last time to see Rome, this dazzling place that left me one friend fewer. Then I headed toward the gate—

"No, I don't have a *passport*! Come on, you know this face!"

I turned back, and there was Lauren. She was holding up the white CELLPHONES IN THE BIN sign like a tall hat. "See it now? Picture this, but, like, on a throne."

I stood frozen in place, shoes in my hand.

"If you look up 'Pope,' I'm literally the first result," she argued. "Definitely if you look up 'Girl Pope.' Look up 'Cute Girl Pope,' I swear—"

"It's okay," I blurted out. "I know her."

Lauren turned toward me. We locked eyes, and shame washed across her face.

"We used to be friends," I said firmly.

The air was thick with tension as Lauren and I walked toward the gate together. Tension *and* mild confusion about the TSA's "vouch for a friend" policy. But as we passed our third Hudson News in silence, I finally came out with, "What are you doing here, Lauren?"

Lauren stopped in her tracks. "What are you talking abou—? I was gonna ask you that!"

"Uh, let's see. You sold me out?!" I shot back. "To the nuns? You told them I hid those vibrators even though *you* gave them to me! I barely *ever* used them."

Lauren's face was blank. Then it softened in epiphany.

"Dude, nooo." Lauren looked relieved. "Some bitch nun found the vibrators when they were cleaning, and I said they were mine. I sold *myself* out."

I jerked back. "What?"

"Yeah, girl. You're looking at an ex-Pope," she said with a little hip pop.

"But I heard, 'Zoe. Zoe. Zoe.' You were saying my name."

"Yeah. 'Zoe had no idea. Zoe should get to stay. Zoe looks great in a two-piece.'"

"Okay, you didn't say that last one."

"I mean, no. But it's true, babe." Lauren gave a smile and fixed the hair on my shoulder.

"But . . . why would you do that to yourself?"

Lauren shrugged. "Let's be honest. I'm not exactly 'Pope material.'"

"Well—"

"And also I'm Jewish."

"I *knew* it!"

"But mainly . . ." Lauren clasped my hand in hers, "because I fucking *hated* who I was becoming to you."

I took a step back. "Your job is more important than me, Lauren."

"Yeah, well, if it's so important, someone else will do it."

Suddenly, the knot in my stomach began to untangle. My shoulders dropped for the first time in months.

"I love you, Zo," Lauren said, pulling me in close. Then she leaned her head on my shoulder as we strolled toward the gate, Italy fading into the background.

"Hey, Lauren?"

"What's up?"

"I wasn't happy for you. I was so, *so* jealous, and I'm sorry."

She shrugged. "I get it. I look great in a hat."

"You do look great in a hat! I've always said that!" We laughed, and I tightened my grip on her hand. "Well, I'm only going to be happy for my friends from now on. I swear."

"Same," she agreed. "We'll probably live longer or something."

I smiled. "Or something."

"By the way, did you hear about Katie?!" she asked.

"No. What?"

"New Supreme Court Justice."

"Katie *Peters*?!"

"Right?!"

"Oh, fuck her!"

"I know, she's gonna drown in that robe."

Fun Guy

You can learn a lot about someone from their relationship with their drug dealer. Are they straight-to-business? Here for a good time? In our case, we buy drugs the same way we do most things: codependently and with shameless enthusiasm. This, in a nutshell, is how any text conversation we've ever had with a drug dealer has gone.

SEPTEMBER 24, 11:28 AM

REBECCA: Hiiii!

Is this Calvin?

SEPTEMBER 24, 1:40 PM

REBECCA: Whoops do I have the wrong number? Haha sorry!

SEPTEMBER 24, 3:27 PM

CALVIN: just woke up

REBECCA: Ah no worries! :)

How are you??

CALVIN: fine who is this

REBECCA: Amazing!! Hope you slept so well

My friend Sarah gave me your number, I hope that's okay

Sarah Statsky

Dark hair

Went to Wesleyan

Claps when the waiter brings out the food

CALVIN: i know her

REBECCA: Crazy bitch, right? 😂

Anyway, I'm working on a creative project (who isn't? lol)

And I'd love to buy some shrooms from you!

Is that something you'd be able to accommodate?

Hello??

SEPTEMBER 25, 2:14 PM

CALVIN: how much

REBECCA: Sorry how much what?

CALVIN: shrooms

REBECCA: Oh sorry when you didn't respond I panicked and deleted the convo

Hahah

But however much you think!

Or is that, like, the only wrong answer?

CALVIN: yes

REBECCA: Well there's just two of us (me and my boyfriend Ben - he's actually also my writing partner. Total Chandler in a Ross's body. Lol.)

So enough for two!

We're not in good shape if that helps/matters

CALVIN: $60

REBECCA: Okay yay!! Do we just Venmo you?

CALVIN: that's fine

will call you about pick-up soon

REBECCA: Ah thank you!!!

SEPTEMBER 25, 2:54 PM

REBECCA: Ok Ben and I are dying at this thought

If I Venmo'ed you and captioned it "drugs"

Everyone would just think we'd gone
to dinner or something

Hahahahah

Okay talk soon:)

REBECCA: Calviiiiin! So great meeting you!

Looping in Ben here:)

BEN: Hey!!! So nice chatting today!

Sorry again about going in for the hug lol

REBECCA: Let us know if you need the info
for the cognitive behavioral therapist
we mentioned

Maybe we'll run into each other
there, ha!

We'll introduce you as our "friend"
don't worry

REBECCA: Bc we're friends now right?

BEN: Calvin fucking Klein!! (don't know your
last name haha)

Naked in the Rideshare   147

Sooo excited for next weekend

Quick question when you have a chance,
know you're busy

Do we have to drug test the shrooms?

> REBECCA: We tried looking it up but couldn't
> find anything and now I'm getting
> targeted ads for Rick & Morty
> LMAO

SEPTEMBER 28, 11:03 AM

> REBECCA: Not that you'd sell us bad drugs
> obviously

BEN: Nooo no no

> REBECCA: You know what? Never mind. I'm
> sure you test your stuff beforehand
>
> Tysm! Will loop back soon!

SEPTEMBER 28, 3:47 PM

CALVIN: u don't need to test

> REBECCA: Okay perfect! Thank you!
>
> Did you laugh at the Rick & Morty thing?
>
> I feel like you did, right??

REBECCA: If not, I can explain it

OCTOBER 1, 4:02 PM

REBECCA: Sarah said she saw you!! Our big weekend is next weekend...!

BEN: (The weekend we're doing the shrooms)

REBECCA: Did you try out the therapist?

CALVIN: not yet

REBECCA: Kk!

CALVIN: my favorite one is the whirly dirly

BEN: Sorry?

CALVIN: my favorite episode of rick & morty is the whirly dirly

BEN: Oh! We don't watch but we will now and we'll start with that one!

OCTOBER 4, 5:12 AM

CALVIN: start at the beginning

BEN: No yeah that makes more sense

REBECCA: Happy S-day!!!

Realizing I should have asked this earlier but how much should we take?

Like a shroom each?

OCTOBER 8, 12:45 PM

BEN: Okay ahhh gonna go for it :)

OCTOBER 8, 1:08 PM

BEN: CALVIN MOTHERFUCKIN COOLIDGE

REBECCA: THESE ARE AMAZING

BEN: BEST PRESIDENT EVER

OCTOBER 8, 2:29 PM

REBECCA: SETTLE A DEBATE FOR US

DO SHROOMS LOOK LIKE ANTENNA?

ARE WE ALL JUST INSECTS WHO LOST OUR WINGS??

WAIT CAN YOU WRITE THAT DOWN FOR ME

CALVIN: no

REBECCA: OK BEN YOU DO IT

BEN: I am in cyberspace send text message please.

REBECCA: BEN YOU'RE ON YOUR
PHONE I CAN SEE YOU

BEN: Get me out of my phone send text message
please.

CALVIN: please remove me from this chat

OCTOBER 8, 4:59 PM

REBECCA: Heyyyy Calvin

Just want to let you know we're one
with nature now

We were telling this tree about you

Wish you could meet it

BEN: Same. Exact. Vibe.

REBECCA: Anyway, we'll tell the universe you
say hiii :)

OCTOBER 8, 5:57 PM

BEN: REBECCA'S GLUED TO THE
FLOOR

ANSWER YOUR PHONE

CALL MY PARENTS 516-487-0194

REBECCA: Hiiiiii!!!! False alarm hahahah

BEN: Hahahahahaha

REBECCA: Okay that was amazing

We didn't get any writing done but we had the best time

BEN: Whoops sorry didn't mean to FaceTime hahah

Call us back if you want though!

Ben Kronengold changed the group name to Shroom and Bored

REBECCA: Omg who did that hahahahahah

OCTOBER 12, 12:51 PM

BEN: Calvin, just want to say our thoughts are with you and your family <3 please let us know if there's anything we can do during this difficult time.

OCTOBER 12, 1:32 PM

CALVIN: ?

BEN: Thought I remember you saying they're from Kansas, read about the tornado there

CALVIN: Minnesota

BEN: Ah

        How are they doing though?

        REBECCA: Do you play Words with Friends

                    Not sure if we can make a three-
                    person game

                    But Ben's calling Zynga to ask lol

        REBECCA: Hey! how much for an eighth of
                    coke

CALVIN: 75

        REBECCA: Jk just wanted to see if you'd
                    changed your number! :)

                    But actually, we want your take on
                    something

BEN: What do you think of this outfit?

CALVIN: please don't send pics

        REBECCA: Oh god because you want to
                    protect our identities?

                    In case things go south?

                    THANK you Calvin

BEN: Hey look at us!

Having ~words with friends~

:)

OCTOBER 20, 12:02 AM

BEN: Hey dude, you still up?

I feel like Rebecca's mad at me

Or not mad exactly, just distant

OCTOBER 20, 12:55 AM

BEN: Has she said anything to you??

I don't want to put you in the middle of this

Like I know you're friends with both of us

But you just know her so well so I thought
I'd ask

OCTOBER 29, 10:01 PM

REBECCA: Did you get married without us?!
You fucking sneak! hahahah

OCTOBER 31, 11:13 AM

BEN: It's not the drugs but the friends you
make along the way

Just thought of that in the shower. Love
you guys.

NOVEMBER 2, 4:12 PM

REBECCA: Calvin. Sarah just told us the news.

We're sick over this and are so sad
you have to move back home

A tornado in Minnesota?

We are actually horrified

Please take care of your (biological)
family

And know your real family is back
here waiting for you

In New York

<3

NOVEMBER 9, 1:03 PM

CALVIN: on 11th and Greenwich ave come out

REBECCA: CALVIN!!!!!!!

CALVIN: wrong number FUCK

REBECCA: YOU LIED????

BEN: WE'LL BE RIGHT THERE!!!!

CALVIN: FUCKKKKKK

How to Get into the Club

1. Enter the hotel.

2. Find the big leather door.

3. Approach the bouncer. Kiss him gently on the forehead.

4. Present ID, then scream, "Don't you know who I am?!" (He won't. Backtrack profusely.)

5. Once inside, find a desk to your left. Do some homework on it. They'll tell you when they're ready.

6. The elevator is a prank. This will make sense when you get in.

7. Get out on the casting floor. Read for a role in Greta Gerwig's new bildungsroman. (You're not supposed to book it—Chalamet's a lock—but it's just good to get in front of them.)

8. Exit through the terrace door. Find Lionel. Lionel is a metaphor.

9. Congrats! You're now in line. Wait three hours and get much hotter to proceed.

10. Speak to the door guy. Break him. Verbally pulverize him.

11. "Sorrrryyyyy." Say it like that. "Soooorrryyyyyy."

12. Get turned away. This is supposed to happen. Find two Daddarios and bring them back through steps one through eleven.

13. Sacrifice the Daddario you're less attracted to. Get biblical with that shit.

14. "Sorrrryyyyy." Say it like a callback. "Soooorrryyyyyy."

15. Enter the club.

16. Find Chet Hanks in an empty void.

17. "The club was the journey all along."
    —Chet Hanks, in the accent.

:(

It Happened to Me:
My Goop Jade Vaginal Egg Hatched into a Tiny White Woman Who I Now Have to Care for as My Own

Let me start by saying this: I'm not usually the type of girl who puts luxury healing crystals up her vagina. But one day, that all changed. A few weeks after my twenty-fifth birthday, I developed the acute and unshakable feeling that my pelvic floor was in need of toning. So in a moment of weakness, I opened my laptop and typed in a search query that would make Gloria Steinem roll over in her townhouse: shop.goop.com. It wasn't long before I was entering my credit card number, weight, and rising sign for a "Yoni Jade Vaginal Egg." I knew I was in for an experience. But I never could have guessed that the egg would hatch into a miniature white girl who I would have to care for as my own. That part wasn't on the box.

Now, in hindsight, I probably could have avoided laying a tiny Caucasian woman. The packaging *did* warn about sleeping with the egg inside of you. But it also said that, in a pinch, I should just watch Gwyneth Paltrow's MasterClass on "Curing Toxic Shock with Positive Thinking," so I wasn't too worried.

I only closed my eyes for a minute, but the next thing I knew, I woke up to the sound of a faint, squeaky "Yaaas" echoing from within me. I looked down, and there she was. This tiny, six-inch-tall white girl with balayage highlights and the smallest Tory Burch bag you've ever seen. Before I knew it, she was stumbling up my chest yelling that her name was "Courtney, spelled the *right way*, bitch!" Then she put us in a group chat called "Slutz," and the rest is history.

Caring for a tiny white woman proved to be a challenge. All day long, Courtney would yell things like, "Food!" "Water!" and "I was born in the wrong era—I should have been a flapper!" Her needs were many, and mostly dietary. She was gluten-free, dairy-free, and an alcoholic. She wouldn't eat animals that were "too cute" or "not cute enough." (We settled on fish, goats, and uglier cows.) And no matter what, at the end of each meal, Courtney would complain that she was "literally huge" and ride off in a huff in her Barbie car.

Then there was her sleep schedule. Despite what Courtney's favorite tank top said, BEDTIME was not THIS BITCH'S BEST FRIEND. Even when I managed to get her tucked in, Courtney would be up for hours because of her "pore anxiety." I even bought her a white noise machine, but she said it was "boring" and "not Drake."

Before I knew it, months went by, and Courtney made herself at home in my apartment. I came back from work one day to see that she had bought a dozen tiny throw pillows that said things like GIRL BYEEE and CHARDON-YAY. Another week she purchased $3,000 worth of gym equipment on my credit card and said she wanted to become a fitness influencer. When I said she was probably too small to work out, she threw the GIRL BYEEE pillow at my head and asked why I hate women.

But I have to admit, there were some bright spots with Courtney too. When my boyfriend dumped me, she put on her sexiest doll clothes and said we were going out. Or when I dropped my favorite earring down the sink, Courtney got inside a condom and let me lower her down the drain to get it. Sure, whenever she got drunk, she would threaten to give herself bangs, but she also once confessed to me that all her friendships felt fake compared to ours. And yes, she had some wild thoughts about vaccines. But needles were big and scary to her, so I kind of got it. I started dunking her in Emergen-C every day and hoped for the best.

And after a while, those good moments began to outweigh the bad. The fighting and bickering between Courtney and me subsided. She started appreciating what I did for her—and everywhere I carried her—and I began to see Courtney for what she was. She was loyal. She had funny observations. She kept the mood up so you didn't have to. And she was actually *really* smart. In her own words, she "basically could have gone to Emory."

I never thought I could like a tiny, six-inch-tall white girl like Courtney. And then suddenly, I loved her. I cared for her, and she cared for me back. I didn't mind if Courtney was "basic." Or if she was born from a pseudoscientific health empire that feeds off women's urge for self-improvement. Because Courtney was so, so much more than that. She really was.

Then one day I woke up and she was gone. The exercise equipment, the Barbie car, even the throw pillows—vanished. All that remained was a tiny note in the most illegible, microscopic handwriting. "Thank you for helping me grow. Thank you for taking me seriously. Thank you for making me feel like I could do giant things." Then I flipped it over. "I DM'ed Drake and he flew me to Toronto LOL I'm gonna ruin him."

The thing is, she was. And he was lucky for it.

Anyway she got squished at the airport. Girl byeee.

The Incident at the Aces Bar

"We never spoke about it after that night. But then again, why would we? It was burned into our collective consciousness. Seared into our very brain matter. No one left that room the same as they walked in. So in a way . . . what more was there to say?"

—PARACHUTE-MAN (PARACHUTE-THEMED SUPERVILLAIN)

The following is an oral history of Scarlet City's infamous "Incident at the Aces Bar." All quotes are taken directly from the supervillains involved, with some paraphrasing for clarity/goblinspeak.

GRAVEYARD, SUPERVILLAIN: Moth-Man was a legend. Let's get that straight. I hated the guy. Tried to bury him alive maybe once, twice a year. But if you say he wasn't a legend, I swear I'll bury you alive so hard . . .

FLYCATCHER, SUPERVILLAIN: We were all shocked when he hung up his wings. Apparently, it was an ACL tear on his way to fight me. Crazy. You hide all these bombs around a public library and then . . . for what?

THE GOBLIN, SUPERVILLAIN: A-gooble-dee-gee! A-gooble-de-ga! Grin-chin-habberdy, doole-de-ga!

(Translation: I heard it was his MCL. Either way, tough way to go.)

MISS BUTTERFLY, SUPERVILLAIN: It was a sexual injury. Greg—er, Moth-Man had a sexual injury . . . I will not be taking follow-up questions.

On the night of February 6, the usual horde of supervillains filed into the Aces Bar in downtown Scarlet City. They didn't know they'd be joined by an unexpected guest.

BRICKHOUSE, SUPERVILLAIN: Brickhouse was playing cards. Brickhouse couldn't believe Brickhouse's eyes when he turn and see Lightning Bug walk through door. Brickhouse say "Go fish" by accident. Everyone laugh at Brickhouse.

PARACHUTE-MAN: Lightning Bug—I can't believe we're even talking about this—Lightning Bug came into the bar. He'd been stepping into Moth-Man's shoes ever since the big man retired. Fifteen years as a sidekick, with just one break in his teens. Maybe for college.

MISS BUTTERFLY: Definitely for college. Bitch walked around with a Princeton shirt under his costume like he was *begging* us to ask about it.

THE GOBLIN: A-rang-tang-tang, feeble-de-gee!

(Translation: Deep down I was always like, we *get it*, you were in an *eating club*.)

Lightning Bug assembled the villains downstairs. They sat around scattered chairs as Scarlet City's new hero took the stage.

GRAVEYARD: And that's when he launched into this whole . . . *thing.*

PARACHUTE-MAN: He was like, "You know . . . It's a new era . . ."

MISS BUTTERFLY: "And I just want to make sure we're being *intentional.* And *sensitive* toward one another . . ." He kept using words like that.

FLYCATCHER: It was weird. He was asking, "How can we be more conscious of *our* dynamic?" Which is like . . . what??

PARACHUTE-MAN: He said he wanted us to feel seen? But also to see ourselves? I raised my hand, like, "Okay, I'm lost."

MISS BUTTERFLY: And then he goes, then he says, "You know, Moth-Man never gave you space to be *you.* For instance," and then he *actually* said this, he goes, "Rainbow Reaper is clearly gay."

RAINBOW REAPER, SUPERVILLAIN: . . . I was as shocked as you are.

GRAVEYARD: And we're all just sitting there like, "I'm sorry, what is *happening*?"

PARACHUTE-MAN: Like, did you just *out* Rainbow Reaper in front of everyone?!

BRICKHOUSE: Rainbow Reaper come out in his own time! We no care! Rainbow Reaper is nicest guy!

MISS BUTTERFLY: And then he turns to me! Lightning Bug turns to *me*, and he goes, "I'm just saying, it's a new world. And you guys still make Miss Butterfly wear a bodysuit." And I go, "*Make?!* Oh, they *make* me?!"

THE GOBLIN: [*eats sheep in disappointment*]

PARACHUTE-MAN: It gets worse from there, but I won't . . . What? You think—you're gonna hear about it anyway?

[*Note: At this point, Parachute-Man left the room, made a phone call, then returned six minutes later.*]

He said we weren't Black enough.

GRAVEYARD: Can you fucking believe that?! He goes, "I'm just saying, you guys aren't the most *diverse* group of villains. Like, it'd be nice to have some Black people in the mix."

MISS BUTTERFLY: And we go, "What? So you can beat them up?!"

FLYCATCHER: "So you can throw them in *prison*?!"

MISS BUTTERFLY: By now I'm losing it and I go, "I'm sorry you're not satisfied beating up poor *white* people!"

PARACHUTE-MAN: Lightning Bug was getting flustered. Yeah. His ears were bloodred. And then he murmured to himself, he goes, "Well, actually, I don't believe in prison, so . . ."

GRAVEYARD: "Tell that to Electric Eel's daughter, you son of a bitch! Tell that to little Suzie Elektrikova who's waiting for her daddy to come home!!"

FLYCATCHER: "Hey if it were up to me," the kid was really floundering now, he goes, "If it were up to me, you guys could do whatever you want!" He says, "You could rob whoever you want. You could *kill* whoever you want—" And we're like, "The fuck are you. EVEN. SAYING?!"

GRAVEYARD: "What do you BELIEVE IN?!"

FLYCATCHER: "It is SO INCONSISTENT!"

MISS BUTTERFLY: And that's when he sort of dug his chin into his chest and whispered, "Guys, like . . . I'm a vegan."

FLYCATCHER: Well, congratu-fucking-lations! You fuckin' maimed Bison-Man, but sure! You're a fuckin' vegan!

PARACHUTE-MAN: "Look!" Lightning Bug screamed at this point. I had never heard him so angry. Honestly.

GRAVEYARD: He goes, "Look! I'm trying to give you guys a voice! And a *platform*! And if you don't want me here, then maybe I should just . . ." And then, I swear to God, he raised his Lightning Launcher to his head.

MISS BUTTERFLY: I mean, what do you say to that? "Noooo. Don't," ya know, "Don't Lightning-Launch your brains out," or whatever. It's always this type of guy, by the way. I saw the "kill myself" thing coming a mile away.

FLYCATCHER: "You're greaaat. We looove you. You were just trying to heeelp." That sort of thing, ya know?

PARACHUTE-MAN: Me, I felt bad for the kid. Because at the end of the day, who *really* needed to feel seen here? Was it us? . . . Or him?

GRAVEYARD: "I just wanted to make a difference," he was saying. He lowered the Lightning Launcher at this point, but shit, was he crying. "I just thought that if I got the job, I could change the culture. And I had all these ideas . . ." Now we all felt bad.

RAINBOW REAPER: "But once you actually get here . . . it's so much harder." He was a puddle at this point.

PARACHUTE-MAN: And then he trails off. Sniffling. And he whimpers, I shit you not, he goes: "I should never have slashed his ACL."

FLYCATCHER: . . . What.

BRICKHOUSE: The.

THE GOBLIN: Rang-tang.

PARACHUTE-MAN: . . . So then we killed him.

FLYCATCHER: Yup! Group murder. How? Oh, we—

GRAVEYARD: BURIED HIM ALIVE, BABYYY! WE BURIED HIM REAL GOOD! DUG A HOLE. BIG HOLE. GOT HIM IN THERE. BURIED HIM. WOO! FUCK YEAH! BURIED HIM ALIVE!

MISS BUTTERFLY: . . . It actually was quite fun.

dating

Fairy God Milf

Bibbidi.

Strange things always happen to me on Sundays. I'm not sure why exactly, it's just something I've noticed. So naturally, it was a Sunday when I first met Belinda. I was nine years old, a squirmy runt of a kid, and she was a talking goldfish who swam up the pipes into my toilet. Pretty strange, even for a Sunday.

"Scooch back, dear," the goldfish said. And before I knew it, there was a toilet-drenched, winged woman sitting on my bathroom counter.

Now you'd think I would've been more surprised to get a fairy godmother. But Belinda had a way of making it feel totally normal. After she dried off, she spent the entire morning walking me through the "rules of wishing." The usual things, mostly—no love spells, no wishing for money, no weird cemetery stuff. And I just sat there like a schoolkid with his new favorite teacher.

In all honesty, it wasn't the magic or the spells that I remember most from that day. It was her sense of warmth. The glint of excitement she'd get in her eyes when I asked a question. The way she rolled her *R*s as she said "ribbety-dibbery" and turned my family cat into a frog. (And then back again. My first two wishes were a bit unrefined.)

All these memories were flashing through my head as I sipped red wine in a hotel restaurant. So many years later, I couldn't believe Belinda's work was bringing her back to Corpus Christi. "Something about the kids down there," she wrote in her email to me.

I had the kind of nervous excitement that makes everyone in the room look like the person you're waiting to see. It didn't matter if it was the bartender or the cactus in the hotel lobby, I kept almost waving hi. (In fairness, Belinda once made herself into a cactus for a Wild West wish, so the cactus thing isn't as crazy as it sounds.)

"I'm sorry," a voice spoke behind me. "I must have the wrong table. I don't remember you wishing to look like Chris Evans."

"You don't?" I asked, eyes still on the menu. "It was right between night vision and flying pony." I turned around and there she was. Iridescent wings. Sun-freckled face and lavender hair. Even for an eternal creature, she hadn't aged a day. Belinda laughed, and we hugged. It was the first smile of a thousand we'd share that night.

It's strange, really. There are only so many magical memories you can keep in your head from your youth. Something about the novelty of a wish-come-true just makes it hard to stick in your brain. Like trying to recall a dream twelve years later. The focaccia bread had barely hit the table when Belinda sent me rocketing back into all these lost adventures. Wishing I had gills at the state aquarium. Turning Ms. Moran into a stack of pancakes during social studies. She even remembered my half-elephant friend, Trix, who I hadn't thought of in years. She thought his name was Trunks at first. We laughed and decided Trunks would've been better.

The night flew by. It was the kind of dinner where we barely touched the food on our plates. The stories kept coming as Belinda walked me to the hotel lobby. Some were hazier than others. For instance, she had completely forgotten about granting me my own boy band.

"We played Madison Square Garden!" I exclaimed.

"No recollection!" she said.

"Trunks was *in the band*!"

She grabbed my arm, hunched over, and laughed through tears.

"Trix, or whatever his name was," I muttered. It didn't matter. We both recovered and took a breath. We had reached the taxi line.

"So," Belinda sighed. "How are your parents? Everyone good?"

"Good. Good!" I said. "They say hello."

Belinda flashed her warm smile, and I offered one back. What followed was the first pause in conversation of the night.

"You didn't tell your parents you were seeing me, did you?"

"No," I answered. "I didn't."

~

Bobbidi.

We made love four times that night.

Three times the normal way, and the fourth as two frost dragons consummating on a cloud. By the time we lay back down in the hotel bed, coated in pixie dust and cotton sheets, I saw my fairy godmother in a whole new light.

"You know, I had never thought about you as a . . . really, I never saw you like . . ." I stammered, wondering why I opened my dry, stupid mouth.

"Oh, you hadn't? Because I've been playing the long game the past twelve years," Belinda laughed back. I was glad she addressed the thing. She was always good at addressing the thing. And then not harping on it.

"So you want to keep those?" She glanced down to the foot of the bed. I still had dragon talons like some kind of magic virgin. We laughed, and she restored my feet with a wave of her wand. And there we were again, not harping on it.

Everyone should sleep with their fairy godmother. It sounds crass, I know. But it's not just the sex that's great. It's that, by the time you're old enough to *have* sex with your fairy godmother, you're old enough to have problems that could really *use* a fairy godmother.

Put it this way: When I was ten, my problems could be solved with a magic snow day. Now, twelve years later, I'm an insomniac with social anxiety and a strained relationship with both of my grandmothers. And Belinda made time for all of it.

That first month, we met up almost every day after work. Always my place—she didn't want to tiptoe around "the new kid." But then again, my place was suddenly a duplex with crystal bidets, so I wasn't complaining. And all those nights we were spending together? They made the hotel rendezvous look boring. We'd get wine drunk and dance the flamenco in my living room for crowds of tiny, cheering Spaniards. We'd watch TV on the couch and teleport our favorite actors to the apartment. We once caught David Schwimmer mid-shit. I swear I've never laughed so hard in my life.

Of course, there was the age difference to consider. I was 24 and Belinda was 5,346. That meant Belinda didn't know all the latest trends. But so what? I told her all about cryptocurrency and front-facing comedy, and she told *me* about how Jesus refused her help that one time.

Then as the nights wound down, we'd lie on the couch, my head in her lap, and I would tell Belinda about my crappy day. She'd brandish her star wand and stroke my hair. "I just wish my boss would get off my case." Boom! Relocated to Chicago. "I wish my lower back would stop hurting." Bam! My back felt better, *and* it apologized to me for the inconvenience.

It was perfect. All of it. And the best part was, I started to learn about *Belinda's* wishes too. It killed me that, in the years I'd spent with a fairy godmother, I'd never thought to ask her about her *own* dreams and desires. Sure, I knew Belinda liked working with kids. But I never knew she used to dream of being a tooth fairy. And that she'd failed her classes because she was too grossed out by the teeth that still had a little gum on the end. I never knew she sewed her dresses by hand, and that she didn't even use magic because she liked the challenge of doing it herself.

Hell, Belinda had a boyfriend the whole time I knew her, and I never even thought to ask! For years she was dating a guy named Cameron Crowe—like the director, but no relation. Think of the laughs we could've had about that! Oh, and my favorite one? Every Sunday, Belinda volunteered at mall fountains, granting wishes to any old schmuck who would come by and flick a penny in. "I just need to hear the words 'I wish.'" She'd laugh. "The pennies are just a bad tip."

It was a different kind of magic. I was getting to know Belinda, and at the same time, I was getting to know a new *me*. What we had—this after-hours relationship—it made me feel like a man. No. Better than that. It made me feel like an *adult*. It didn't matter who was mad at me or what I messed up at work or what girl from high school ignored me on the subway. At the end of the night, it would all be fixed. And even better, I was going to fall asleep next to my *fairy godmother*. She wanted *me*. How many people can say that?!

"What did I do to deserve you?" I would ask her at three a.m., hands pulling at my hair, all worked up. "You shouldn't be with me. You should go be with Poseidon. Or—or Shrek! Is Shrek real?!" I'd rant. But she'd just laugh, and laugh, and smoke her magic wand from the non-star end. "I wish you'd never left," I'd say, turning to her. "But if you had to go, you came back at the perfect time."

Then my mind would wander off, and I would get lost in some worry. A shitty thing a friend said. A coworker I had accidentally upset. The typical crap of life. And Belinda would roll over toward me.

"Tell me," she would say. "Your wish is my command."

"So, Belinda!" my mother exclaimed, holding out a platter of cocktail shrimp. "How long are you in town for?!"

Belinda and I stole a glance across my parents' living room.

"I'm here to stay!" Belinda answered. "New assignment's out in Rockport."

"Is that right?!" My mom gave a little clap. "Well, good thing you and David bumped into each other!"

"Your new kid as much trouble as David was?" my dad asked from his armchair.

"Ha! No, he's good! He's sweet! Petey Weissman," Belinda nodded. "Keeps wishing for a tail, but . . . No, yeah, it's a little weird."

"Hey, do you remember . . ." my dad began, straightening his reading glasses. This could go in one of a million directions.

"David was ten-ish and still keeping you a secret from us, and we come back from dinner one night—boom, there's David, ass naked in the dining room." This was the worst of those one million directions.

"Oh *yeah!*" my mom joined in. "He said he was 'getting to know his body,' but really it was a . . . what did you call it, David?"

"An invisibility spell, Mom. And it wore off as you walked in. And it's very funny," I snipped.

"You know, the other day I found this drawing from fifth grade," my mom went on, like someone was paying her to torture me. "And it was a drawing of David and this—this *fairy* woman. And when I asked him about it, he said to me, 'Mom, that's my girlfriend!'" My parents cackled. "But it was just you!"

"Smooth, David!" my dad added.

"And let me tell you, B, he drew you with some *big* . . ." My mom cupped her chest and puffed out her lips, taking all the known ways you can traumatize your adult son and compiling them into one gesture. I was cosmically nauseous. I just barely mustered up the courage to glance up at Belinda. She couldn't even make eye contact with me.

"You know . . ." My dad leaned in. "When we *did* find out about you, Belinda, I was . . . I was too harsh."

"Oh! Tom, you were *fine*," she insisted, looking into her drink. "Everyone reacts differently to—"

"No, no," my dad pushed. "I overreacted. I was too fixated on

David growing up the 'old-fashioned way,' whatever that means. But looking back, I was wrong. You were great for David. Gosh, you were like a second mom!"

I could see Belinda's ears go red from across the room.

"Well, thank you," she offered.

"Plus, it's more common than I thought! The fairy godmother thing," my dad said. "This guy in my office? He grew up with one too!"

"Oh yeah? What's his name?" Belinda asked.

"Cameron Crowe. Like the director, but no relation." And my stomach sank into the floorboards.

Boo.

"You DATED him?!" I shouted across my apartment. "You dated your FAIRY GODKID?!" I was blacking in and out of my body.

"When he was thirty!" Belinda yelled back. "What, now we're judging dating fairy godkids?! Because if we are, I've got news for you!"

"Obviously, I know *I* was your godkid, Belinda! But I thought I was the only one you—"

"I've had thousands of kids!"

"And how many of them have you slept with?!" I yelled. Then, silence.

Belinda stared *through* me. Then she snapped her fingers and disappeared into a cloud of glitter. It could've easily been smoke too. But she knew I'd have to clean up glitter.

The next few days were excruciating. There's no other way to describe it. Belinda and I weren't talking. The only palatable minutes were the ones when I first woke up, before everything that happened came flooding back to me.

To make it even more painful, without Belinda there, all the crap of life went completely unchecked. I scheduled a company-wide meeting on Labor Day, and I couldn't wish it fixed. I missed my niece's birthday, and I couldn't wish that better either. Even my apartment was back to normal. No crystal bidets to speak of.

It all just felt so complicated. And for what? I'd spent my whole childhood fixing my problems with silly rhymes and magic dust. Why couldn't I just have that again? I resented sex for messing up my relationship with Belinda. I resented Cameron Crowe—the guy, not the director. And mostly I just felt profoundly stupid. Before this, in my lowest moments of our relationship, I was worried I was using Belinda. To solve my problems. Or to make me feel like a grown-up. But I never considered she was using me back. In a strange way, it made me feel better. It also made me feel so, so much worse.

I sent Belinda an email a week after the incident at my parents' house. It took some convincing, but she was open to talking. She made me promise to never question her professionalism as a fairy godmother again. I agreed, and she poofed over a few seconds later.

What was supposed to be a "quick chat" turned into an hour. Then two, then three. We talked calmly, then we raised our voices, then we sat in silence. Then we got back into it again and repeated the cycle. One second I was sure we were mending things. The next, I was certain we would never even look at each other again. Eventually, we took a break to have sex. I don't think either of us felt great about it, honestly. But we agreed it might help lower the temperature of the situation.

As we lay in bed together afterward, a sense of finality hung in the air. It was like the answer was handed to me. We couldn't go back to what we used to be. And I don't mean twelve days ago. I mean twelve years ago. What we had now just felt wrong. A rotting taxidermy of what we once were. It felt gross, and sad . . . and I felt gross and sad.

"I think . . ." I turned to Belinda, readying myself to do something I never could've imagined just days ago. "I think we have to call it, B."

She rolled her eyes and turned away. But I put my hand on hers and moved closer. "I hate it too. Believe me. I hate myself for this. These last few months have felt like a gift, having you back."

"Don't."

"I want it to work. But we both know . . ." I trailed off. "We both know."

Belinda stared at the comforter. "I don't know how it got so complicated."

"Me neither. Believe me, me neither. I'd kill to go back to when it was simple. Without sex, without anything. Like it first was, when I was nine and you were a goldfish swimming around my toilet bowl. But we can't go back, B. I *wish* we could, but it just can't happ—"

"Every. Single. Time," Belinda sneered. Her voice shifted. Lowered. I had never heard her sound so . . . cold. Her posture straightened as she looked at me with a sorry smile. "How many times are we going to do this, David?"

I felt my heart pound. I didn't know why.

"How many times are we going to meet in that hotel bar? And reminisce about all those stories? It's just so *predictable*."

My eyes widened. "What?"

"How many times am I going to invite you up to that hotel room?" She sighed. "It always starts off great. Then a few months pass, and you lose your nerve because of . . . *something*. And then you *wish to go back*. To when it was simpler. Easier. So . . . let's *go back again*, David." Belinda pulled her wand out of thin air.

"No. No no no, I didn't wish for—!"

"But you just did. You *wished* we could go back."

My body shut down. All the blood rushed to my head.

"And your wish . . ."

"Holy shit, holy shit, don't send me back—!" Instinct took over. I grabbed a pen off the nightstand.

"...IS MY COMMAND..." she roared.

I lunged for a scrap of paper, scribbled something down. I crumpled it into my hand. "Don't—!"

"See you in the bathroom, David."

Bibbidi.

Strange things always happen to me on Sundays. I'm not sure why exactly, it's just something I've noticed. And this Sunday was no different. I was nine years old, a squirmy runt of a kid, and I woke up with a scrap of paper crumpled in my hand. That was all that happened this Sunday so far. But still, pretty strange. Especially because there was just one word written on it.

FLUSH.

Sex and Love in the Alien Invasion

Well, ladies, it's been five months, three weeks, and six days since the Tryxlobytes made contact with Earth. And lucky for you, we here at *Cosmo* are already experts on fucking and sucking them. So sit back, strap in, and set phasers to vibrate, because we're giving you the terms and tricks you need to know to get *probed* this post-invasion. Let's dive in.

Glossary of Terms

AGE OF TRYXLOBYTES: Refers to the new era that began when Earth joined the Federation of Planets on behalf of the Tryxlobyte Empire.

Ex. The Age of Tryxlobytes seems scary, but with 41,622 new terrestrial species to fuck, I never have trouble getting action!

ANIKA LOWELL-SCHWARTZ: The first human to imagine sexual exploits with the invading extraterrestrials. Considered the "Jane Goodall of railing aliens."

Ex. I'm just grateful Anika Lowell-Schwartz got day-drunk and admitted, "Okay, but those aliens could get it, right?"

ATTRACTR: Popular dating app connecting young singles on the same planet or asteroid-province.

Ex. We have to make you an Attractr. You just swipe left for no, and swipe right to be lifted in a tractor beam that brings you face-to-face with your match. Watch. *AHH!!!*

BURROWING: When a size-altering species such as a Burant or Grozok shrinks down and enters their partner whole-bodied. Also known as *Richard Gere–ing*.

Ex. Sorry if I—*mmm*—seem distracted, you guys. This Grozok I met last night is still burrowing in me. You're doing great, Cooper!

CLONEPLAY: Use of Dualgaxian technology to create duplicates of oneself or one's partner, often as an anniversary sex thing.

Ex. At brunch, Bridgette told us the cloneplay was great, but that afterward both duplicates claimed to be her real husband, so she shot Josh's clone, she thinks.

EXTRASPECTING: Refers to a pregnancy with a fellow member of the Federation of Planets. Derived from *extraterrestrial* and *expecting*.

Ex. I was shocked when my oldest friend Jenny showed up to

brunch engaged and extraspecting. "The doc says it'll be a classic chestburst delivery. I'm gonna be a mom!"

THE FISHBOWL: Refers to a popular nightclub where guests consume Polyscales, transferring their consciousnesses into insatiable fishlike creatures.

Ex. It felt weird going to the Fishbowl without Jenny, but I actually met a nice Glorxian guy who took the form of a gorgeous sea dragon. We banged fin all night!

FISHHOOKED: Refers to falling for someone you met at the Fishbowl.

Ex. My friends all said, "We told you so!" when I mentioned I was getting dinner with the same Glorxian guy I met at the Fishbowl. "You're fishhooked, girl! Go get him!"

GLORXIAN CATCH-ME-UP: A telepathic download of your new partner's memories to avoid the whole "how many siblings do you have?" thing.

Ex. Chad, the Glorxian guy, transferred his memories into my head before the salads even arrived. I guessed right. He *was* cool in middle school.

HOME-PLANETING: Bringing your partner on a trip to your home planet, often to meet family. Considered a "big step."

Ex. It felt a little fast to go home-planeting to Glorxon, but something inside of me said I should finally put my walls down for this guy.

HOME-STRANDING: Being left on a deserted planet by your date, often as a form of ghosting a new relationship. Considered a "big trick."

Ex. I thought Chad was going to refuel the ship, but then he never came back. My heart dropped into my stomach. I was being home-stranded.

JANKLOBAITING: The act of wondering aloud, "Is the Janklian Church of Space Christ taking new members?" in order to lure the Janklo people into portaling to your location so you can get a ride home.

Ex. I had to Janklobait my way home, Jenny! They spent the whole time trying to Space Baptize me! This is why I don't do relationships!

NINTH-DIMENSIONAL PORN: Erotic mind-technology that places users in their wildest subconscious fantasy.

Ex. I'm telling you, Jenny, this website is broken. The ninth-dimensional porn I clicked on kept showing me growing old with someone I care abou—Ohmygod, nooo.

TRUE LONELINESS: The cosmic feeling like you're alone in a universe with 41,622 known species who aren't choosing you.

Ex. I mean . . . Why didn't you tell me you were engaged? Why didn't you tell me you were *pregnant* and engaged, Jenny? I didn't even know you were seeing someone. We're supposed to be best friends, and I had to find out with the group?! Do you know how that made me feel? Like—screw getting home-stranded. *That's* true loneliness.

UNAPOLOGETIC: Refusing to acknowledge or express regret.

Ex. Jenny said, "I didn't tell you because you're constantly shitting on relationships! All you talk about is sex, and the latest 'sex terms,' and how love sucks. And honestly, I don't know if you really feel that way, or if it's the sex columnist talking, or if you're just clinging to this persona you've created because the only thing scarier than the world right now is being alone in it. But I'm not alone anymore. And maybe that just means we're fundamentally different." Then Jenny left, unapologetic.

UNBURROWING: When a size-altering species such as a Burant or Grozok exits their partner's body and grows to their full size, sometimes after weeks pass by.

Ex. Hey, I'm so sorr—Cooper here, by the way. I am *so* sorry it took me so long to unburrow from you. I was stuck up there like you wouldn't believe. But first off, fuck that guy. Fuck that guy who left you on that fucking planet. He sucks. And second, I'm sorry about your friend Jenny. That must feel really shitty, too. But for what it's worth, you're *not* alone. You weren't alone this entire time, and . . . You know, I really didn't mean to eavesdrop. I'm not saying that *I'm* right for you. Or that you even have to look at me ever again. But, if you wanted to grab lunch sometime . . . I'd be excited to *actually* get to know you.

YEAH: Taking a chance; keeping faith in the universe.

Ex. Yeah. I could grab lunch.

Clarity

Love is a promise. But every promise . . . comes with a journey.

I nestle between my sisters in a soft velvet box. Their names are Pear Shaped and Cushion Cut. Above us, a man with teeth as white as pillows presents us to a boy.

"They're beautiful," the boy says. In this moment, I know. He is about to make a promise.

The boy picks up Pear Shaped. She shimmers in the light.

"Do you think she'd like that one?" the man asks.

"I don't know." All the love is making the boy's skin moist. He picks up Cushion Cut in his other hand. "What do you think?"

"I'm just the host, my man. You have to let your heart lead the way."

The boy looks at Pear Shaped. Then he looks at Cushion Cut. Then he looks down on the table . . . at *me*. "What's this one?"

The Host Man's smile gets wider. "Princess Cut."

I am Princess Cut. The boy lifts me in the palm of his wet, love-soaked hand. For the first time, he smiles. It's a forever kind of smile. "This is the one."

The Host Man beams back. "And you're one hundred percent sure about Rachel A.?"

The boy nods. "I love her more than anything in the world." He looks off. A forever look in his eye. "These have been the best five weeks of my life."

~

It's dark in the box. But after every darkness . . . there's light. The boy's proposal will come just after "last looks." From the sound of it, "last looks" are beautiful. All the love is making the boy jiggle his leg. I bounce around his pocket. Then, finally, footsteps.

"Hi." The boy's voice cracks.

"Hi." The next voice is higher. It's Rachel A.

His leg stops jiggling. He takes a breath . . . and he makes his promise.

"Rachel A., I didn't know what to expect from this journey, but it's been amazing. From the moment you stepped out of the limo, I knew we had something, like, just amazing. I love the way you make me laugh. I love how fun you are on helicopters. I even liked your family. So . . ."

And suddenly . . . light. I peek out of the box and gaze upon the most beautiful woman I've ever seen. She's beautiful because she's in love. Sometimes love can take your words from you, and Rachel A. can hardly speak. She shakes her head up and down.

"Yes! Shut your face. Yes! Shut your fucking face." She could have said it one thousand times.

I'm placed on Rachel A.'s beautiful finger. Her hands are shaking with the promise of a lifetime. "It's so heavyyyy!" She grabs him, and I brush against the boy's face. "I'm engaged, bitch!"

He and she become we.

～

Bryan and Rachel A. are holding hands. They angle their love toward a woman in a headset.

"So while the show is airing, no posts, no telling friends, no ring in public. K? Stay in your house in Chicago." *Chicago.* It's where he's *from*. Once I asked Pear Shaped where we're from, and she said we're not supposed to talk about that.

"What about public sex? Is that okay?" Bryan asks.

Everyone laughs. Bryan is the funniest man in the world.

～

"Welcome home!" Bryan tells Rachel A. as they step into their forever apartment.

We all walk around together. "It's not exactly the mansion," he tells her, taking a pair of sweatpants off the stair rail. She smiles a soft smile.

"No. But it's perfect."

～

We stay in the apartment for most of the daytime. We cook food that burns and sing songs in the living room. One time I fall into the toilet by accident and Bryan fishes me out with salad tongs. It was scary, but love can be scary, and also I'm fine and don't want to talk about it.

One night, Bryan smiles at Rachel A. His smile is worth a million tomorrows. "I hit 100K on Insta."

Her face lights up with even more tomorrows. By the sound of it, this is the most beautiful news in the world.

~

We sit on the couch and watch Bryan and Rachel A. on TV. She holds his hand and he squeezes it whenever they are on screen. A forever kind of squeeze.

One week they are in a castle in Italy eating spaghetti under the moonlight. Rachel A. sighs and says she misses those nights. Bryan looks concerned. But concern . . . just means finding a way through.

The next day Bryan orders pickup from the "Red Lobster." It comes in big plastic boxes. He is excited. Rachel A. and I come downstairs, but she says, "I'm allergic to shellfish."

Bryan looks surprised and says he didn't know that about her. But I'm not worried because getting to know you . . . takes a lifetime.

~

Rachel A. is twisting me. Tonight on TV, Bryan is going on a date with Mykayla. They kiss and Mykayla says that she is falling in love with him. Bryan says it back.

Rachel A. is not holding Bryan's hand now. Instead, we are tapping on a big glass of wine like strong, clinky women. "Why don't you call her up?"

"Babe." Bryan holds his head in his hands.

But Rachel A. is on her phone. "Twitter loves you together. I say go for it."

We spill the wine a little. It's messy, but sometimes love is messy.

Mykayla is wearing a lot of rings. Whores.

~

Next week Bryan sends Mykayla home. Rachel A. stops twisting me so much.

Mykayla cries in the limo. But tears just mean you care, and Mykayla clearly cares so much she tricked Bryan into saying things to her like "I'm falling in love with you."

Bryan puts his arm around us. Now on TV, Bryan and Rachel A. are riding donkeys in the Grand Canyon during sunset. It is a memory worth engraving. I wonder if Mykayla will ever get to ride a donkey with someone. Everyone deserves their donkey person, even if they are crazy and trick people.

~

"For the first time together, America's couple: Bryan and Rachel A.!"

We walk out together and Rachel A. waves. I reflect the bright lights onto a crowd of cheering faces. The people smile and woot. This is what their love does. It makes them woot.

We sit on the couch across from the pillow-teeth Host Man. "What a proposal," he says, dabbing at his eyes. "Don't you guys think?"

The people cheer even louder for their love. Off to the side with the other women, Mykayla claps her whore rings together. She's not smiling because her trick didn't work.

"So, Bryan, Rachel A., what's next for you?"

Rachel A. looks at Bryan. "Honestly," she says, "we're just ready to live a normal life."

"Well, we wish you all the best."

~

Normal life *is* the best. Every day we go on TV and talk about our love. At night we go to fancy restaurants "on the network." Bryan and Rachel A. are very happy, and I haven't been twisted in a while.

The people we meet in front of the TV cameras are beautiful like Bryan and Rachel A., except they are old (thirties) and smile but not with their eyes. They ask Bryan and Rachel A. about babies. Bryan says, "Soon," and Rachel A. says, "What?!" and they all laugh very hard. Rachel A. is the funniest person in the world after Bryan.

At night we do sponsored ads. Bryan and Rachel A. talk at their phones about skinny teas and fiber powders and other gifts they are sent because they are a perfect couple and people like them to poop good. One time Rachel holds up a wine and says, "Bryan and I drink this every night after dinner, and you won't believe what it does to us in the bedroom."

"Makes me pass out cold," says Bryan. She pushes him hard. "BRY-an! Now we have to start again."

~

Tonight we are getting dinner with Stacy A. and Allegra. Stacy A. is Rachel A.'s sister, and Allegra is her wife. I do not know what show they met on.

Rachel A. and I arrive first. Bryan comes later because he needs to be on an important work podcast.

"It's so great to finally meet you, Bryan!" says Allegra.

"You too!" says Bryan. "We missed you during Hometown Week."

"I know," Allegra says. "I just kept thinking what my partners at the firm would say if they saw me on, like, a dating show . . ."

"There are only so many decorative candles Allegra and I could take," Stacy A. says.

We all laugh, but Bryan doesn't laugh with his eyes. I wonder if the TV people taught him that.

"So how's living together?" asks Stacy A.

"It's been great! A little cramped," says Bryan. "We'll probably get a new place by the time we're officially the Poulters."

Stacy A. laughs. "As long as you're not actually changing your name, Rach," she says and sips wine.

"Oh." Rachel A. clears her throat. "Yeah, I'm still deciding."

"What—?! Come on!" Bryan says. "You really want to keep 'Ainscough'?"

Rachel A.'s face turns red. I didn't know *A* stood for "Ainscough." Maybe she didn't either.

"Actually, it's *'Ayns*-cough,'" Allegra says. "But glad you two are so close."

Bryan jerks back. "I'm sorry, did I do something wrong here?"

Rachel A. kicks him under the table. Her pulse races. It tickles.

"What?! I'm just asking. Did I do something wrong?"

~

That night I go flailing as Rachel A. shouts that Bryan embarrassed her.

Bryan says that those people made him feel like an idiot. He says he's "sorry I'm not a fucking lawyer, Rachel. I worked at a gym before this. If that's not good enough for you, I don't know what to say." Neither do I, but luckily no one asks me.

Rachel A. pulls at her hair and I am almost tangled. "That is not what this is about!"

"So what is it about?"

"It's that you don't know anything about me!" she yells back. "It's like there was no *me* before the show! And now there never *will* be, because I left my job, and my city, and I'm giving up my fucking name now?!"

"That's marriage! That's what you wanted!" Bryan says.

"*Is* that what I wanted?!" shouts Rachel A. And then we leave the house all dramatic like when Paige G. got sent home for drugs.

~

I am splashed with tequila. Most of it is in Rachel's mouth but a lot gets on me too.

Rachel slams down her glass and the girls at the bar cheer. They are her "friends from home," so their skin is bad and none of them know Andy Cohen. Rachel A. looks happier than I've seen her in a while.

"I say dump him," says one of the friends from home. Then she looks around the bar and says it again more quietly. "I say dump him and go back to your old life. You were in *vet school*, Rach. You don't need to be promoting teas for a living."

"Completely agree," says another friend from home.

"Blegh," says the third friend from home. She is not adding to the conversation because she just stopped breastfeeding so her tolerance is low.

Rachel A.'s eyes widen. "Shit." She jumps off her stool and ducks behind her friends. "That's Lexi."

"Lexi?"

"She won Kevin's season. Hide me."

Her friends mush together into a big friend hiding wall. It only works for a second because Lexi comes over.

"Oh my God, heyyy!!"

Lexi has the tallest shoes in the world. She has a giant sparkly ring too, so she must be in a lot of love.

Rachel A. changes her face from wants-to-hide to happiest-ever. "Lexi! Oh my God! I thought you and Kev were—"

"In Portugal! We were!" Lexi turns her head a lot like someone is taking pictures of her but no one is. "We came back early. Couldn't make content at the hotel because vibes were wrong. You get it!" Maybe Rachel A. gets it. I do not. "But how are *you*, girlie?!" she asks. "Is it so crazy? Engagement can be sooo hard."

"Oh, I'm actually really glad you said that," Rachel A. says. "It can get intense, right?"

"Ohmigod, *totally*," says Lexi. "The amount of time Kevin spent in LA while I was here in New York? Wild."

"Really?!"

"Yes! He's literally there right now. Probably with Marni from Eric's season, or whoever he's fucking this week."

Rachel A. looks shocked. "Wait. You guys split up?"

"Oh my God, never," says Lexi. "And break the fans' hearts? No way."

Rachel A. cocks her head. "But you just—"

"I'm just saying, girl, I know what you're going through," she says. "It's not our fault they only cast douchebag narcissists for the lead."

Rachel A. looks confused. Like she is maybe thinking about the donkey ride and the Red Lobster and the laughing.

Lexi leans in. "All I'll say is this." Then Lexi looks at *me*. "You only need to stay together for two years to keep the ring." She taps her finger on me. "Ride it out, then *cash* out. That's happily ever after, girl."

Then Lexi leaves in her giant shoes.

~

That night Rachel A. comes home and lies in bed. We think Bryan is sleeping because he looks like he is sleeping.

"I'm sorry," Bryan says, not sleeping.

"Me too," Rachel A. says. She stares at the ceiling.

"This is all just so much pressure, you know?" he says.

"I know."

They lie in silence. Then finally, Rachel A. stands up and turns on the light.

Then . . . she takes me *off*. She holds me in the palm of her hand. Bryan looks sadder than I've ever seen him. But Rachel A. doesn't look sad at all.

"Let's get rid of it."

~

Bryan digs a hole in the backyard. Rachel A. lays me in it. I am scared. I worry that it's a forever kind of hole.

But Rachel A. and Bryan are holding hands now. "Should we . . . like, say something?" he asks.

Rachel A. looks at me. Then looks back at him. "Bryan, I didn't know what to expect from this amazing journey. But this journey has been amazing. And from the second I stepped out of that limo, I knew something amazing was in store . . ."

He laughs and shoves her a little. I remember this speech from the first time I met them, at the start of what was supposed to be their forever.

"Let me start over," she says and goes "ahem." "From the night we met, to the moment you asked me to marry you, one thing was certain: we were surrounded by fucking people."

"And cameras," he reminds her. "And producers, and the director's nephew who picked out the bikinis, and—"

"He did?!"

"Yes! Why do you think I canceled the pool date?"

"I didn't know!" She laughs. Then they sigh. I am still worried because the hole.

Rachel A. takes a deep breath. "I thought I wanted to spend the rest of my life with you. And I think I still do. But . . . honestly? The rest of it stresses me out. So with that in mind. Bryan?" she asks. "Do you want to just date?"

Bryan smiles, tears in his eyes. "I very much want to just date."

They turn to me. Then they wave goodbye.
I am covered in dirt. It goes dark.

~

That night, Bryan digs me up and puts me in his sock drawer.
"For one day."

~

One day hasn't come yet. But a lot of other days have.

I can't see much from inside the sock drawer I am kept in, but sometimes I get bumped around and can see outside the keyhole. Bryan and Rachel A. laugh, and sometimes cry, and play drinking games to other seasons of the show. They fight about work stuff and who killed the plant and they say sorry and I love you. One day they come back with simple rings on their fingers. They seem boring. But they seem okay.

The Reynolds Accords

As comedy writers and skilled practitioners of asskissery, we sometimes find ourselves getting to work with well-known actors and celebrities. Over time this becomes normal, just another part of the job. (No it doesn't.) But every now and then we find ourselves working with someone so special that we're forced to think about . . . contingencies. The following is a contract we drew up in the event we ever work with one Ryan Reynolds.

THE REYNOLDS ACCORDS (the "Reynolds Accords") are entered into as of the 18th day of July 2023, by and among Ben Kronengold ("Participant") and Rebecca Shaw ("Cute Participant") and serve as a binding agreement in the unlikely but cataclysmic event that they are invited to have a threesome with Ryan Reynolds ("Yes, That One").

1. Initiation. Following the completion of a successful day of comedy with Ryan Reynolds, Parties are advised to stay alert to "sexy vibes or innuendo" given off by Ryan Reynolds. Such vibes include, but are not limited to, prolonged eye contact, flirtatious stretching where Ryan Reynolds's sweater

rises a little and you see the hair under his belly button, and/
or the question from Ryan Reynolds, "Would you like to
both have sex with me at the same time?" (the "Offer").

2. Deliberation.

    (a) Weigh Factors. Upon extension of the Offer, Parties
    must give a valid excuse to exit the room.[1] Parties then
    must weigh the following factors:

        (1) Jealousy Factor. Would either one of the Parties
        become exceedingly jealous over the course of
        the threesome? Would such jealousy negatively
        impact Parties' relationship long term, and would
        such devastating impact be outweighed by getting
        to kiss Ryan Reynolds on the body and face?

        (2) Prank Factor. Are Parties considering the
        possibility that this is, in fact, an elaborate
        prank being pulled on them, judging solely by
        the implausibility of Ryan Reynolds wanting to
        make love to them specifically? Are the Parties
        weighing the chance that this is perhaps a very
        expensive Cameo their friends have hired as a

---

1   Example excuses to leave the room may include, "Do you hear that? I think
it's my doctor in the next room." Or, "Do you smell that? I think my doctor in
the next room may be on fire." Parties may also feign a spontaneous game of
Hide-and-Seek, provided Parties can really sell it.

joke, or an episode of *Punk'd* where the catch is that they're pranking people who are not famous but *were* the stars of their respective Bar Mitzvah seasons?

(3) <u>Bloating Factor.</u> Has either one of the Parties eaten anything bloat-inducing in the past 12 hours, and if so, why would one of the Parties do that on such a big day?? When Parties might have sex with Ryan Reynolds?!!!

(4) <u>Future Sex Factor.</u> Are the Parties considering the effect sex with Ryan Reynolds might have on sex with any other non–Ryan Reynolds entities going forward? Namely, that Parties will spend the rest of their lives chasing this high, always pursuing but never truly capturing the ghosts of what was? Or something.

(b) <u>Thinking Faces.</u> After discussion of the above factors, Parties will make convincing thinking faces for 3–5 seconds then immediately agree to have sex with Ryan Reynolds.

3. <u>Procedure.</u>

(a) During the Activity, Parties must do their absolute best to be really, really good at the sex, i.e., anniversary sex, not *Succession*-is-on-in-the-background-and-we're-both-wondering-what-Tom-got-up-to-this-time sex.

(b) Less-Cute Participant aka Ben Kronengold may not, under any circumstances, panic and fall into an Obama impression during Activity like he did the first time Cute Participant said "I love you" in bed. Less-Cute Participant may, however, begin Activity by politely "drawing a line at guy-on-guy stuff, not that I'm judgmental, it's just not super my thing" but reserves the right to promptly reverse his stance mid-Activity upon realizing, "Holy shit, holy shit, it's Ryan Reynolds naked."

(c) Cute Participant, on the other hand, may do sex to and with Ryan Reynolds in any and all agreed-upon capacities, but must pretend afterward to Participant that she "didn't even have that much fun." She is required to glance over at Participant every so often and mouth, *Overhyped*, even if on the inside she is experiencing the godly eruption of a Pleasure Vesuvius. As Activity goes on, Cute Participant is encouraged to resist her natural urge to micromanage, suggest overly ambitious positions, and/or stop the Activity to check if anyone wants snacks.

(d) Parties are forbidden from the following: (i) asking for Marvel spoilers, (ii) saying "thank you" too much, and (iii) mentioning that there was a contract. The last item is punishable by death.

4. <u>Postprocedure.</u> Following the Activity, Parties are at liberty to snuggle in bed together, interlace fingers, and discuss what Blake Lively is like in real life. (4–5 questions maximum.) Cute Participant may now get snacks, specifically frozen pizza, cutely quipping as she reenters that she's "sorry it's not *licorice* pizza," before Less-Cute Participant shoots her a look of "Stop, he wasn't in that, that was Bradley Cooper." Following an appropriate post-lovemaking period, Parties will collect their things and leave in a Lyft, or whichever ride-sharing app has done something terrible least recently, since that seems like the kind of thing that Ryan Reynolds would care about.

5. <u>Confidentiality.</u> In lieu of the common nondisclosure agreement, the Reynolds Accords include a unique and highly specialized "yes-disclosure" clause. In the months following the Activity, Parties will do their best to drop whenever possible that Parties made love to, with, and on top of Ryan Reynolds. To avoid risk of social repercussions, this will be done through graceful segue. Acceptable transitions include:

(a) "Wait, speaking of *Deadpool*, you guys know Ryan Reynolds?"

(b) "I'll have three pumps of caramel, please. You know what else is best in threes? Genitals. When one of them is Ryan Reynolds's."

(c) "Let's play a game. Touch your nose if you've ever had sex with Ryan Reynolds at the same time as someone else."

IN WITNESS WHEREOF, the Parties hereto have executed, however overly optimistic, the Accords as of the day and year first above written.

Rebecca Shaw
Rebecca Shaw

Ben Kronengold
Ben Kronengold

Soulmates

After twelve long years of love and partnership

The day is finally here

Mr. and Mrs. Fudderman and Mr. and

Mrs. Peña joyfully invite you to celebrate the wedding of

their children

Bryce Louis Fudderman

and

Anya Beth Peña

Saturday, October 21

4 PM at Eastville Gardens

See warnings attached

Warnings

Hi. So obviously it's been a while since most of you have seen Bryce and Anya. They've gotten weird. Let us explain.

After twelve years of spending all their time together, Bryce and Anya have picked up quirks that range from unlikeable to *Shining*-twins disturbing. We've gotten used to it, but these changes may be jarring if you're one of the many people they've alienated over the years. Some things right off the bat:

- Bryce and Anya have become unsocialized. Like the opposite of those animals you see on The Dodo. Do not approach one without the other present, which they will always be, unless they are walking down the aisle or actively taking shits.

- Many couples start to look like each other after a while. In Bryce and Anya's case, they've actually started to look like a third person: Q from *Impractical Jokers*. This is not a value judgment, nor is it a dig at Mr. Q. It is just the truth, and you should be prepared.

- Bryce and Anya now get dressed "drawer-blind," i.e., they pick their clothes from either one's wardrobe without discrimination. Last month Bryce wore a crop top to his nephew's bris. It was progressive and forward-thinking but mostly just bad to look at.

- Finally, Bryce and Anya will leave their own wedding early to stretch each other out. We wish this were a euphemism. Every night Bryce and Anya wear matching American Eagle sweatsuits and stretch each other's quads, backs, and hamstrings thoroughly. Passing gas is not only permitted during this process, it is, regretfully, encouraged.

A Note on Chester

To avoid confusion, **CHESTER IS A DOG.** You may hear Bryce and Anya refer to themselves as "parents," "Chester's birth parents," or "in a throuple with Chester." They do not have a child, nor are they polyamorous, though they did once have sex with Chester on the bed. They will likely work this into their vows.

Topics to Avoid

Since many of you will be speaking to Bryce and Anya for the first time in years, here are topics to steer clear of:

- Bryce and Anya's cabaret classes. **Do not get them started.** They are *mean* in cabaret class. If you are flat, they are mean. If you are late, they are mean. If you are not off book by show week, they will comment mean things on your granddaughter's Instagram until you are memorized. Do not take the bait if they say something like "Do you know the musical *Tootsie*?" or "Want to hear about this cunt Doreen?"

- Similarly avoid ANY TALK OF SLEEP HABITS. They are volatile. Since 2012, Bryce and Anya can only fall asleep if they are cuddling "hole-to-hole." Also, every night they participate in a phenomenon called Sleep Tank, wherein they pitch "the Sharks" ideas and inventions, in tandem, while unconscious. The sight is disturbing, and the idea is almost always "salad phone."

- There is no other way to put this one except to say we lied before and they have taken a shit in the same toilet at the same time. Do not poke this bear.

Groomsmen and Bridesmaids: Please Review This Part Carefully

We are depending on you all to ensure a smooth wedding week.

Attached below is the wedding party list. If you are included in the wedding party but unsure why, just remember that *this is what happens when you find your partner in eighth grade and decide you're done meeting new people.*

GROOMSMEN: Adam (groom's brother), Ryan (groom's brother's friend), Chester (still a dog), Chester's dog walker Rick

BRIDESMAIDS: Hot cousin Stephanie, Nana Marilyn, Mrs. DiMarinis (Anya's fourth-grade teacher), Chester again

Despite our best efforts, Bryce and Anya will be having a joint bachelor-bachelorette weekend. There will be couples' charades. You may think you have to let Bryce and Anya win couples' charades, but rest assured *they will win no matter what you do*. One family game night Anya made a face, and Bryce guessed "Meghan McCain's cornrows" correctly. This will also be worked into the vows.

**We as parents are split on this next point, but the moms think it'd be good for Anya to "catch some dick" on her bachelorette weekend. The dads remain dick hesitant/generally dick wary.

Conclusions

Finally, we understand if you draw the following conclusions about Bryce and Anya after the wedding weekend:

- They are agoraphobic.

- They are in a two-person cult.

- They speak solely in inside jokes, and you are one of those inside jokes.

- They would have just eloped if it weren't for Mr. Fudderman's insistence that a big wedding would be a "great chance to woo Shanghai."

- They need to see a therapist. Not the therapist they've both been seeing but entirely new, entirely separate therapists. Plural.

- They are perfectly matched soulmates, and any of us Bryces would be lucky to find our Anya.

Thanks.

We'll see you at the wedding.

the real world

Actual Things Ben's Mother Has Told Her Friends He Does for a Living

"He's pre-premed."

"He's a *FAKES COUGHING FIT*—ologist."

"He *says* he writes comedy, but I read this article about how a lot of the CIA types use cover stories, so fingers crossed."

"He works for Jimmy Fallon. As his tax attorney."

"He's playing an elaborate, five-year-long prank where eventually he'll surprise me with a business degree and a grandchild."

"He's a trial lawyer. He tries my patience."
   (Usually followed by:)
"That was funny. You should use that in one of your little skits, Ben."

"He's a rectal doctor. Yeah, he thinks it's a little embarrassing, so he'll tell you he writes comedy."

"He's a senator. What, Miss Fancy over here knows ALL the senators?"

"You know Banksy? . . . . I'm just saying, it's possible."

"He was his middle school valedictorian. Oh, you mean since then?"

"He's an MD."

"He's a PhD."

"He's an MD-PhD for the ACLU, *dayenu*."

"He works for a nonprofit. Because he doesn't make a profit."
   (Usually followed by:)
"Ronnie, text that one to Ben. See if he likes it better than my trial joke."

And finally, "Who's Ben?"

Sky Not Found

In 2009, in a small suburban town, a life-sized error message appeared in the night sky and sent an entire community into panic. Look it up. The picture you'll find is completely real.

This account of what followed afterwards is real-ish.

~

Celia Berry wore her prom dress to the town hall. After hanging in her closet for twenty-three years, it fit just the same as it did back then: boxily. The crowd around her droned with anxiety as Celia hummed ABBA to herself in the first row. In a tidal wave of fear and existential angst, Celia was the sunglass-wearing sea turtle riding the foamy crest.

"Okay, listen," began Mayor Ned Zelzer, a small-government man with a big-government podium. "We've heard reports of this 'error box' over Fairhaven last night." This was already a departure from how Zelzer normally started his town halls: by cough-stalling until someone else took over. "So for those of you concerned, please step up to the microphone. And then after that we'll—*achem*—decide on how to—*achem* . . ." He trailed off, eventually mumbling, "Well, no spoilers," before inhaling a Ricola and sitting back down.

Now, there are a lot of problems with opening a forum to a town of four hundred. But the first thing you'll notice is the overlap. There are only so many cultural references a group of people can make when they all skimmed the same books in high school. Town pharmacist Harold McCraw hit the big ones off the bat. "Is this some kind of Big Brother shit?" he asked. "Or are we maybe in a *Horton Hears a Who!* scenario?" In the crowd, scores of disappointed townspeople crossed off their own talking points. "I'd also just like to add . . ." McCraw leaned into the mic. "*The Matrix. The Truman Show.* And the weird one with the hot pale twins."

"Really?!" "You took all of them!" "That last one's just the third *Matrix*!" The town was already growing frustrated, but the reality of what was happening to Fairhaven had only begun to set in.

"If you ask me, we're in some kind of computer simulation," insurance agent Peter Flounder said into the mic. "And it seems that simulation has an error. Now, what happens when a computer has an error?" Nervous chatter gripped the room. "It can reset. It can shut down. It can . . ." He jolted into a robotic pose. ". . . *Freeze*??!" A gasp or two from the back. Peter Flounder was also the local thespian, which you could tell from the little bow he took before sitting.

"Ellen?" Mayor Zelzer looked into the crowd. "Does that check out with your computer expertise?" Fourth-grade typing teacher Ellen Rover tapped her chin in the first row. Then she did some air-math, pretended to carry a one, and gave a firm nod of affirmation. The tension slipped into panic.

"Carlton Grocers will be shifting to surge pricing!" announced Jen Carlton. "Like Uber, but you'll starve."

"The Hart family is sheltering in our motel!" declared Herbert Hart. "All adulterers out by noon. Sorry, Lowell." Lowell's wife choked on her water.

"If we're gonna Purge, I'd rather know now, K?! 'Cause I will blow up ALL you cocksuckers!" announced Pastor Jeremy. The room erupted in a pre-Purge kind of way.

"Excuse me? Hello?!" A small voice rang through the noise. Thirteen-year-old Agnes Packer stood up from her seat. "Maybe the question here, dear Fairhavenites, isn't 'Are we real?' or 'What might happen to us if we aren't?'" she offered softly. "Maybe the question is: 'How do we come together when we're forced to question everything?' Or, 'Can we find purpose in ourselves even when we don't know what "self" is?'"

A long pause.

"Oh, screw off, Agnes!" a crowd member yelled, followed by an echo of cheers. Agnes was always saying stuff like this and, frankly, it was annoying.

"Settle! Settle down!" called out Mayor Zelzer. "The sheriff and I will decide on a plan of action. We hear you all loud and clear, except for one of you, obviously." The mayor stared at Agnes until her eyes dropped to the floor.

"Hi! Hello! Just one more thing!" Just then, middle school

chorus teacher Celia Berry shuffled to the front of the room. Her pink ruffled train flounced behind her. "Oh, no thanks. I don't need that." She rejected the microphone. "*Achem.* BEFORE WE ALL LEAVE!!!" Celia bellowed. She really should have taken the microphone. "WHO HERE ACTUALLY SAW THE ERROR MESSAGE?! WITH THEIR OWN EYES?!"

Celia looked out into a still crowd. No movement. Then she raised her own hand, dumb-proud like a pageant winner. Another hand followed. Then another, then another. A total of six eyewitnesses in the crowd. Then one final hand poked through the back row: twenty-four-year-old Molly Gage. The recent college grad felt a swell of stares and clenched her fist in regret. But she had already been counted.

"Eight. Okay. CAN THE EIGHT OF US MEET OUTSIDE WHEN THIS IS OVER?! K, THANKS!" Celia left the podium and strode down the aisle with confidence, accidentally high-fiving someone who was just stretching. "Whoops. Well, here take another." She doubled down and made it ten.

The rattled crowd slowly rose to its feet, as seven souls followed a grown woman in a prom dress out the door.

~

"Molly! MOLLY! We're over here!"

"Shit." Molly slowly turned in the courtyard. She'd been trying to slip out with the crowd, but Celia Berry had eyes like a hawk.

"You coming?!" Celia called out, hustling past local reporters.

"How are you? Dad good? Good, I'm glad." Celia rushed through the niceties. This was, after all, the apocalypse, maybe.

"Yeah, everyone's normal." Molly brushed her hair back. She had a residual teenage angst that, at its best, read as worldliness.

"We're all meeting at my house to talk about what we saw," Celia offered. "See if we can put any clues together."

"Oh no, I shouldn't," Molly interrupted. "I'm leaving town in a day or two. Just back visiting. So I shouldn't get too . . ." Molly trailed off and gestured vaguely. "Involved."

"Oh. Okay!" Celia said, pretending like this computed to her. "Well, to each her own!" The two women stood in silence, Molly crushed under the weight of Celia's genuine smile. "Hey, if you change your mind, I'm making a Lay's chip casserole!"

"Nice."

"I'm sure everyone's hungry. I know I haven't eaten since I saw the *G-L-I-T-C-H* in the *S-K-Y.*" Celia pointed up and smiled.

"Cool. Well, thanks." Molly turned to leave, then she caught a glimpse of the other six witnesses and stopped short.

"What? What's the matter?" Celia glanced back. "You friends with one of them?"

"Hm?" Molly refocused. "Oh no. Just—I know the tall one from high school."

Celia beamed. She liked when people knew each another.

Molly's eyes stayed locked on a six-foot-one twenty-something fielding questions from reporters. "Actually, will you text me your address?"

~

"It was nuts! I mean, it was only up there for a few seconds. Not even enough time to take a picture. But *whew!* It was like God was connecting to Wi-Fi, and the bitch forgot his password."

"Right?! Agreed." Celia paced around a circle of folding chairs in her living room, peeling a barcode sticker off an unused serving platter. "And so where were you when you saw it, Bradley?"

"Well, me, I'm an early riser," Bradley Prince-Phierson continued. "So I was getting things ready for the shop, icing a carrot cake, and *bam!* I saw it right out my kitchen window." Bradley was well known in town for his gay-weddings-only bakery. Then when that didn't yield enough customers, he expanded it to "gay parties" and "gay business meetings," which just meant anything in sales. "It gave end-of-the-world vibes, for sure. Then my cake started sliding and I thought, '*Dear God, fingers crossed!*'"

"Innnteresting," Celia said, emptying a bag of tortilla chips into a bowl. "See, for me, I got more of an inside-a-video-game feel. But no, this is good, let's discuss."

"If it helps to know what I was doing," high school sophomore RJ Poster offered, grabbing a fistful of chips, "I was on the porch texting my girlfriend. She's pretty cool, I dunno, you might know her from movies."

"Um, what?!" Celia exclaimed.

"Yeah, it's not a big deal. She's just—" RJ presented his phone, and the whole room cringed.

"Oh, that's . . . Well, sweetie, you're not actually—" Celia stammered as RJ swiped through photos.

"So that's Gal Gadot," Bradley said bluntly.

RJ sighed like he knew this was coming. "Please, *please* don't tell anyone about us, guys. Gal says she's visiting next summer, but I don't want, like, everybody in town talking about it before then. Okay? We have enough to worry about now."

Bradley blinked. "Uh-huh, so you're getting catfished—"

"AHH, and who's next?!" Celia swooped in, lacking the courage to break such a dumb heart. "Patty? Tom? You guys wanna go?"

But before they could answer, the back door slammed. "*Shit.*" Molly crept in and sat down, wearing a much cuter outfit than she'd had on at town hall. "Sorry." The room paused for her. "Sorry. Go."

Lawyer Patty Violet went next, hand in hand with her husband. "So I saw it. Tom didn't," she began. Tom Violet was already shaking his trucker-hatted head in frustration. "Sorry, it's just—it's difficult for Tom because of the *reason* he didn't see it."

The group leaned in.

Patty sighed. "We were making love. And in the position we were in, I was able to see through our window, but Tom—wasn't."

"I see—"

"It's called the Amazon position!" Patty burst out.

"Why?! Why does this have to be our story?!" Tom wailed.

"It's where the woman is on top," Patty went on, "and the man is beneath her, stretching his legs all the way up. Almost like the woman is penetrating him with his own penis—"

"Whoa!" "*Oh*-kay!" The group tried to drown her out.

"So that's the truth!" Patty pushed on. "I was able to see straight ahead, out the window. But Tom was looking up, through his own legs, at the ceiling."

"It's a sick joke!" Tom cried out. "Now every day people will be asking me, 'Oh, what were you doing at that exact moment, Tom?! What were you doing right then when the world stopped working, Tom?!' And I have to tell 'em this shit?!"

The group sat in stunned silence.

"You could've said you were sleeping, dude," Molly said.

A longer pause.

"GODDAMNIT!" Tom stomped his foot and threw his chair over.

"Jack! Hey! Jack! Your turn!" Celia improvised a quick tune, one of her many chorus-teacher strategies for pushing through discomfort. Then the lanky twenty-four-year-old from the courtyard cleared his throat. Molly glanced up.

"Oh yeah. Mine's just like everyone else's," Jack said. He had a mumbly, deep-voiced quality about him that shouldn't have worked, but it did. "I was playing basketball in the driveway and, like everyone said, it was right there in the sky. Really freaky." He turned to the woman next to him. "How about you, Mrs. Lasseter? How did you see the error message?" Molly zoned out again.

Libby Lasseter was the last to share. She was Fairhaven's resident PTA pitbull, known for her signature gold sequined journal and her reputation as a "real pants-shitter" by the local teachers' union. "2:43 a.m.," Libby read from her journal, "I was checking over Opal's math homework. My husband, Darryl—owner of Darryl's Gyms and Day Spas"—she looked around importantly—"was asleep. And suddenly I was illuminated by this . . . *presence*. I looked up. Through our skylight . . ." Libby shuffled in her seat, drew a sharp breath. "And that's when I saw it." Her voice betrayed her, giving out. "Four words. I could just make out four of them."

A sudden gravity fell on the circle. A tightness of breath. Like they were all silently begging her not to read on.

"Error: Sky. Not. Found." Libby gave a small shrug and forced a smile through misted eyes. "That's what it said. Sky Not Found." Libby closed her sequined journal and exhaled.

"That's what I saw too," Patty added quietly.

"Me too," said Bradley. He put a hand on Libby's shoulder. It was suddenly much graver than a story, more terrifying than a sharing circle. They'd all returned to that moment of cosmic loneliness.

"Hey! Well, hey, don't get down about it!" Celia squeezed between chairs into the center. "We're the lucky ones, guys. We *saw* it!"

"No," Libby said emphatically. "We weren't *supposed* to see that. That was something—not meant to be seen." The group sat in tacit agreement.

"*Pffff.*" Then Molly burst out laughing. "I'm sorry. Sorry," Molly mumbled, collecting herself.

"What's funny?" Celia turned, genuinely hoping something was.

"No, it's just—this. This is funny." Heads cocked around the circle. "Like, I'm sorry, you guys are just—the *most* precious. I'm remembering this next time someone says *my* generation's too sensitive. God."

Bradley the baker bristled. "I'm sorry, are you not taking this seriously?"

"Yeah. Jeez, aren't you scared?" Patty asked.

"Um, okay. I'm twenty-four," Molly answered. "I'm *only* scared. Like, all the time. But that's just—that's part of it! I dunno!" She threw her hands up. "I've been *deeply* prepared for the end of the world *since* I was a toddler. I've literally had to be. And if what we saw up there is the world ending?" She shrugged. "Could be worse."

"How could it be worse?" Bradley snipped.

"Um, it's better than a climate crisis?" Molly answered. "It's better than—fucking nuclear war. Or, have you guys read about superbacteria?! If there's a glitch in the Matrix, then at least that sounds instant. I mean . . ." Molly laughed to herself. Then a less kind thought struck her. "And if I'm being really honest, this is probably good for you guys."

"Good for us—? Okay, what is your problem?" Libby shot back.

"I'm serious! Like, what a distraction!" Molly said. "What a thing to talk about in town! This is huge for Fairhaven, culture-wise." She lost the whole room on that one.

"Um, Molly? Honey?" Celia kept the peace. "Some of us are questioning whether we're even real here. Ya know?" She winced.

"And if we're not real?" Molly shrugged. "So say we're not real. We're not real, and now we're talking about it. It's just a thought experiment. Like, it's a privileged problem. What does it change for you, actually?"

"Okay, *I'm* real!" RJ spoke up.

"Fine! Sure!" said Molly.

"And so is my girlfriend!" he tacked on.

"Oh, sweetie, no . . ." Celia moaned.

Molly exhaled and walked around her chair. "Look, if it makes you feel better, I'm leaving in a day or two and returning to a world with, frankly, much scarier problems."

"So why even come here, then?!" Bradley demanded. "Why show up?"

"Uh, to fuck *him*! Obviously." Molly's hand swept across the room. All eyes slowly, cautiously followed—and landed on Jack. Silence.

"Oh, grow up," Molly scolded. "We've all fucked. It's not like I want to Amazon position him."

Patty's husband buried his head in his hands.

"What—? Sorry, you came here to—?" Jack stuttered. "With me?" Jack suddenly became aware of his posture.

Molly rolled her eyes like it was obvious. "You were cool in high school and now I'm hot and went to college."

A pause. Jack rubbed his jaw, taking this all in. Then approximately half a second later: "Great, I'll grab my stuff." Jack hurried to the door, and Molly followed. "Thanks so much, Ms. Berry!"

"Wait. Wait, wait. You guys can't leave! We haven't put any clues together yet—!" Celia called after them. But Jack was already wrestling his shoes on.

"Damn, Molly. That was some deep shit. I forgot you were a genius and stuff." Jack hopped on one sneaker.

"I read, like, one article once. Calm down." They descended down the porch stairs. Gone.

"Wait, I made a—" Celia started.

Ding! The kitchen timer rang.

"Lay's chip casserole," Celia said under her breath. No one had ever said those words so sadly.

~

In the days that followed the town hall, a new kind of Fairhaven started to take shape. Talk of the error message dominated every conversation, replacing the usual subjects of school events, weddings, and the Great Bulging of '11, wherein local bookseller Greg Garrett may or may not have had a Coke can in his pocket twelve years ago. But beyond shifts in conversation, the very fabric of Fairhaven was starting to fray. Local businesses were hit hardest. The few store owners who stayed open in lieu of spending time with their families were plagued by looting, theft, and vandalism, mostly by said families. Divorce rates spiked, especially once the bowling alley announced its new role as an end-of-world sex club with different lanes cordoned off so you don't run into your cousins. Gyms disappeared overnight. No one seemed upset about that.

As for the townspeople themselves, they fluctuated between despair and absurdity. Faced with his newfound meaninglessness, for instance, Mark Mackley proclaimed himself Fairhaven's new mascot, wore nothing but a dog collar, and relieved himself in public twice daily. After a week of doing this without the reprieve of an apocalypse, Mark Mackley posted a lengthy apology to the town Facebook group and politely asked to be reinstated as school principal. His decision was still pending.

The one person who managed to stay above water, it seemed, was Celia Berry. After looping the other seven witnesses into a group text, Celia immediately set about recording everyone's birthdays and food aversions on a whiteboard labeled MYSTERY GANG. She placed a decoupaged tip box on her front lawn for additional clues, dutifully sifting through it at the end of each day. And other than adding R.E.M.'s "It's the End of the World as We Know It" to the sixth-grade choral rotation, Celia remained pretty unfazed by the maybe-end-times. She still woke up each morning with a smile. Still started her day with her skin-care routine. As far back as she could remember, in fact, Celia had the same exact face-washing ritual: 1) rub bar soap onto face, 2) stick whole face under faucet, 3) drown self, just a little, 4) dry off with funny "This Side's for My Ass" towel, 5) finish with a leg pop. After all, Celia arose each day to a world that still existed, and that meant a leg pop was in order. But on this day in particular, it also meant screams of:

"WHERE IS SHE?!"

"COME OUT HERE!"

"WHAT DO YOU HAVE TO SAY FOR YOURSELF, CELIA BERRY?!"

Celia rushed to her front window. "What in the . . . ?" She peeked out the glass.

"I SEE HER!"

"SHE'S COMING OUT!"

Celia unlocked her front door and stepped out into bedlam. Flashing cameras. A mob of reporters. Microphones thrust in her face. Protestors with CONSPIRACY and WHY ARE YOU LYING? signs lined her lawn. Celia knew all the protestors personally too, and had gone to grade school with most of them, which made for a lot of "Seriously, Lisa? You could've just called!" But one reporter's question pierced through the noise.

"What do you have to say about the Libby Lasseter allegations?"

"The what? What allega—I can barely hear you!"

"Libby Lasseter's allegation that you made up the error message."

Celia heard *that* perfectly. And all the commotion around her faded into a shrill ring.

"*What*?"

~

"'So do I think our world is malfunctioning? Did I really see some kind of *giant warning sign* over the town that night?'" Libby read from her signature sequined journal outside of town hall. "'No. Absolutely not. But out of concern for our town, I *pretended* like I saw something to gain the witnesses' trust. My thanks to Peter Flounder for the acting lessons.'" Local thespian Peter Flounder took a tiny bow beside her. "'Now for those of you who want the truth," Libby announced, "here it is. These 'witnesses' have no evidence. No consistent story. The Error Message Hoax is just that. A hoax from within. And our town is the victim of a conspiracy.'"

Reporters erupted with questions. Libby's husband and former gym owner Darryl Lasseter stepped forward, calling on them one at a time.

"The fuuuuck?" Molly grumbled in her car, eyes studying Libby on her phone screen. "She *did* see it. I heard her whole story."

"Mm. Mom never liked that woman," Molly's dad muttered from the driver's seat. "You know, Libby Lasseter wins Best Gazebo in town every year. No one else in town even has a gazebo," he pointed out. "She should also win Worst Gazebo." Bill Gage had a gruff indignation to him, about everything, always.

"This is wild." Molly stared out the car window. Protestors picketed by town hall. Counterprotestors marched across the way. Up ahead, shoddy graffiti reading THE END IS ~~NIGH NEIGH~~ NEAR dripped down a now-shuttered bodega. Molly felt a pang of nausea.

Naked in the Rideshare   233

"You saw what you saw, Mol." Bill bit into a granola bar. He pulled up to the curb and kissed Molly on the head, mouth still full of oats. "What were you gonna do? Shut up about it?" Then Bill opened the car door and turned to the sea of reporters at town hall.

"Wait, where are you going?" she asked.

"I want to tell them that I'm Batman."

"Daaaad!" Molly moaned.

"I'm going to work! Relax! I'm cutting through Delancey to Main Street."

Molly rolled her eyes. Then she unbuckled her seat belt and folded herself into the driver's seat.

"I'm not gonna try to stop this," Molly said out the car window. "I don't care enough."

"Good. You shouldn't," Bill answered.

"Let everyone here think I'm a liar. I don't care."

"Great. Don't care."

Molly shifted. "But like what if I can find *proof* of the error message—"

"Oh, well, there's an idea!" Bill exclaimed, giving her the hint of a smile. "Seat belt," he said, tossing Molly the car keys. "Will try to leave work early tonight. I'll bring you home a gay cake from Bradley's."

"Dad!!"

"What?! You want a straight cake? I thought you were

tolerant." Then Bill cut through Delancey to get to Main Street, leaving Molly's mind to race.

~

"So my parents aren't talking to me . . ." RJ sighed at a picnic table in Fairhaven Memorial Park. The rest of the witnesses sat around him. "The vice principal sent me home from school today until 'further notice,' but I can't go back home because of all the protestors outside my house." RJ stared at the ground, then lit up. "So, yeah! No parents, no school. Been a pretty sick day!"

"RJ! No!" Bradley said like he was dog-training. "This isn't a joke. You get that there are literally calls to *disbar* Patty?" Patty sat farther down the table, ghost-pale. "I can't even get into my bakeshop because of the picketers, and people are boycotting the fire department because of Jack."

"Wait, Jack's a firefighter?" RJ asked.

"No!" Jack burst out. "I've just *called* the fire department before. This fucking town, I swear to God." Jack paced around.

"Okay! Hey! Hi, guys!" A winded Celia hurried toward the picnic table. "*Whew.* So I've been digging around . . ." Celia threw a thick stack of documents down on the table.

"What's all this?" Jack's eyes narrowed.

"*This*," Celia answered, "is how we prove we're telling the truth." The group crowded around the pages. "This is every article, every note, every description of what we saw that night," Celia explained. "Our proof is in here. We just have to find it." She held up a printout. "Like, look! This? This is a map of all our houses. Notice anything?"

They all studied the map. Then Celia drew a line connecting their homes. She held up the abstract shape, manic.

"You *guys*. It's a friggin' dino nugget!" Celia slammed the map down. "I mean . . ." Celia held her arms wide. "Could that be anything?!"

The group's spirits sank, their spark of hope extinguished.

"It could also be a dino-*saur*?" RJ stared at the map.

"Nuh-uh." Celia glanced down at it. "No, I don't think so."

Slam! Out of nowhere, a notebook flung through the air and hit the table, skidding off the wood and onto the grass. The group startled.

"Ugh." Molly's voice followed. Then she trudged toward the group, picked up the notebook, and placed it back on the table.

"Jesus, Molly!" Patty caught her breath.

"I think I shit my sundress." Celia craned back to check.

Jack stood up, leaning into Molly like they were the only ones there. "Hey, so the other night was amazing," he whispered. "You know, my parents are looting the hardware store later if you want to come to my place—"

"Shh. Shut up."

"K, cool." He sat back down.

Then Molly nodded to the notebook she threw. It was familiar, covered in gold sequins.

RJ looked at it. "Wait, duuuude!"

"Is that—?!" Bradley realized. "Is that Libby Lasseter's journal? Well, there's our proof!"

"No."

"Oh."

"I bought this at the stationery store just now. But it's the exact *same* journal Libby has," Molly explained, hating how deep into this she was. Then she unzipped her backpack and shook it over the table. Six identical journals fell out. "If we really want to prove that we saw something that night . . ." Molly began, "then all we have to do is swap out one of *these* for Libby's journal. And we'll have our proof."

Eyes lit up around the table.

"Wait a second," Celia paused. "We're not *stealing* someone's property."

"Fine, don't. But all of Libby's notes are in her journal. She wrote down everything she saw that night," Molly insisted. "It'd be Libby's word against her own."

"No. No." Celia shook her head. "No, yes. Yes. I came around to it." Celia let out a little squeal. "Are we really gonna do this?"

"The woman's lying! We have to defend ourselves," Jack chimed in.

Looks of resolve around the table. A desperate, clinging confidence.

"Okay, I hate to be all—" Bradley interrupted, turning toward Molly, "but I don't trust you." Bradley shrugged. "I don't. Why'd you come find us? I thought 'nothing mattered' and we're probably not even real."

Molly sighed. "But you're still the realest people I know." She paused. Then she burst into laughter. "Kidding. I'm just fucking with you. But no, this town is becoming more insufferable by the minute, and I still have to visit twice a year. K?" Molly grabbed a notebook and walked off. "See you tonight. Wear heist clothes."

"Tonight?" Celia thought aloud. "What's tonig—Ohhh." Then she remembered that they lived in a small town and there was probably a fair tonight.

She would probably be right.

~

Say what you will about the town of Fairhaven—its people, their divisions, its one restaurant, the way its toilet bowls fill with gasoline unless you flush them to the rhythm of "Don't Go Breaking My Heart"—but they know how to throw a damn fair. Tonight was admittedly different, though. The fracturing of Fairhaven into what people started calling the "Bufferers," those who believed reality was malfunctioning, and the "Truth-Tellers," those who believed nothing but were much better at naming things, made for a tense event. Nevertheless, at a quarter to eight, Molly, Celia, and the rest of the witnesses entered together through the balloon arch, all with vastly different interpretations of "heist clothes."

"Is that . . . ?" A darkly clad Jack studied Celia.

"Yuh-huh, it's an *Ocean's 8* shirt," Celia smiled. "They had a heist. Rihanna planned it."

Jack nodded. "Cool."

Down the line, Molly was focused, carnival lights bouncing off her face. She scanned the group for everyone's decoy journals. Check. "Stay alert," Molly told them. "Find Libby, swap the journals, get the proof." Molly surveyed the fairground, an endless maze of bodies and colors. "And if the world ends before we get our evidence . . ."

"Then it could be worse," Celia jumped in. She turned to Molly and smiled. "It could be a superbacteria." Molly, despite herself, smiled back.

"Ready?" she asked.

"Ready," RJ called out.

"I'm ready." Jack nodded.

Bradley gave a thumbs-up.

"Then let's—!"

"Oh, crud. Where'd Tom go?" Patty looked around for her husband. "I coulda sworn he was just—"

"EAT SHIT, UNIVERSE!" Tom's voice boomed from above. *BLAM! BLAM!* The witnesses swung around to see Tom, from atop the Ferris wheel, blasting a shotgun at the open sky. Screams broke out across the fair. "YOU THINK YOU CAN MAKE A FOOL OUT OF TOM VIOLET?! I'M AN AMAZON, BITCH!"

Molly and the group stared up slack-jawed, half in shock, half hoping Tom might hit some kind of artificial screen in the sky and do their jobs for them. But there was no strange impact. No chunk of the heavens falling from above. Just an entire fairground sent into panic as a sexually mortified husband shot at the clouds.

Now generally speaking, a fair is not an easy place to find someone, but a mass exodus makes it that much harder. "Go! Now! Find Libby!" Molly yelled as a sea of people rushed toward them. Within seconds, Celia was swept up in the fleeing crowd of people, jolted around, and deposited in front of the Hall of Mirrors. Once inside, Celia began her search for Libby, emerging an hour later with nothing to show except a discovery about the true meaning of beauty. So, there was that.

For his part, Bradley managed to escape the throng of people. Thinking fast, he boarded the Gravitron for a better vantage point of the fair, not realizing the Gravitron was a fully indoor ride that spun him forty miles an hour and made him call the ride operator the C-word.

Luckily, though, RJ was able to easily maneuver *through* the crowd given his small frame. Unfortunately for the group, RJ got quickly distracted by a fair exhibit called "Fairhaven and the Onion Famine." RJ was curious by nature, and also two of the onions looked like breasts pushed together, so it really was a perfect storm.

And that meant Molly was their only hope. Across the

fairground, Molly ducked and weaved inside the frenzied crowd. She could barely see past the flailing limbs, only catching glimpses of the tent tops above her. But one banner caught Molly's eye. FAIR-HAVEN'S BEST GAZEBO. Her breath tightened. *It was the Lasseters' tent.* With pure instinct, Molly *flung* herself out of the mob and landed in front of the pavilion. She glanced up . . . and Libby Lasseter and her husband stood just feet away. Libby's sequined journal protruded from her bag. It was Molly's for the taking.

Then Molly heard a deep voice. "So yeah, I just thought you should know."

"Oh my God, thank you for telling us," Libby responded.

"We won't let anything happen to it." Libby's husband took the journal out of her bag and ripped out the pages, a dozen at a time.

Molly's stomach dropped. Standing across from the Lasseters— was Jack.

"*No.*" Molly stood up. Jack went pale at the sight of her. "What did you do?"

"Molly, I'm sorry—"

"I could have you arrested!" Libby warned her.

"Oh, suck an ass, Libby!" Molly snapped back. She turned back to Jack in anger. "Why? We had a plan. Why would you tell them—"

"Because I didn't see it!" Jack blurted out. "Okay? I didn't see it, Molly!"

Molly staggered back. "*What?*"

"I didn't see any kind of error message. Or—or sign in the sky. I went to bed at ten o'clock that night. I didn't see shit."

"But you *said* you saw it."

"Yeah!" Jack shrugged. "People say stuff. I don't know, maybe I wanted to feel like a part of something. But I didn't think it would ruin our lives, Molly!" Jack's eyes darted around. "Like, are you sure *you* even saw it?"

"Oh my God," Molly turned away.

"Seriously! What if you made a mistake?! It was three in the morning; you were probably half-asleep!"

"No, actually I was smoking a blunt in my dad's hot tub. Like a fucking champion."

"Ohh. Okay!" Jack held his hands out. "So you were high. You were high and you saw a sign from above that the world was ending. And you're sure about that?"

Molly stared through him. Then Jack's tone shifted.

"We can take it back, Molly," Jack pleaded. "I'm going public with this. I'm saying I didn't see anything. Just do it with me."

"But I *saw* it!"

"So just say you didn't! Who cares?! We can put an end to this!"

"But why would I lie?!"

"Dude, because you have a family?!" Jack fired back. "This is real life! Don't you feel bad for your dad?"

Molly recoiled like Jack had slipped into a different language. "For my *dad?*"

"You're okay with him losing his job over this? That's really worth it to you?!"

Molly's face contorted. "Okay, my dad's not *losing his*—"

"He did! This week," Jack said. "He did."

Molly froze. The air around her went thin.

"No one wants anything to do with us, Molly. My mom too, she—there are consequences for this shit," Jack said.

But Molly just stood there, eyes glazed over.

"You—you didn't know?" Jack murmured.

Molly didn't. But now that she thought about it, you couldn't cut through Delancey to get to Main Street.

~

The crowd of fairgoers clustered in the parking lot, still panicked from the gunfire. Celia, a stuffed penguin under her arm, spotted Molly seated on the curb and beelined over. "So?! How'd it go?!" Celia offered the stuffed penguin. "I stole this. You want it?"

Molly didn't reply. She just stared off, knees pressed to her chest.

"What? You couldn't find Libby?" Celia asked. "Darn. Okay, maybe someone else in the group did."

"Celia . . ."

"You know, I bet RJ found her. He's slippery. In a moist teen sort of way."

"Celia."

"Or Bradley could've—"

"I'm telling everyone I made it up."

Celia blinked, trying to understand. "You're what?"

"I'm telling everyone I lied. About the error message. So that'll be it. This all . . ." Molly gestured around to the crowd, to their palpable anxiety. "It will all be over."

Celia's head shook automatically. "But you didn't lie."

"But maybe I did!" Molly threw her hands up. "Like, I don't even—I was fucking tired. And *high*. And maybe I just thought I saw it once I heard other people did. I don't know! I can barely remember anymore."

"Okay, *skrrr*, dim the gaslight." Celia sat down next to her. "Molly, you *saw it*. Don't second-guess yourself. Second-guessing is for tax forms and deciding whether there's a little bit of cross-walk in the Captcha thing. That's it."

"But we don't have proof," Molly stressed.

"So?! Who needs proof?!" Celia burst out. "Let them think we're crazy. Something is *wrong with this town*. We can figure it out ourselves if we have to. Us and the gang!"

"Jesus! There is no *gang*, Celia!" Molly shot up. "You're like— you need this. I get that. You need this for yourself so badly. But it's fucking ruining people's lives!"

Celia jerked back. Molly realized she'd gone too far.

"I'm sorry. I didn't mean it like—"

"No. You're . . ." Celia thought hard. "I mean, I didn't think I 'needed' this, but . . . Crap." Her wheels turned. "I mean, maybe you're right. Maybe I should say I was lying too."

"What—" Molly froze. "You're serious? Just like that—"

"Well, if it's messing up people's lives, then yeah," Celia reasoned. "Plus, I trust you. And you made the same call, right?"

Molly's eyes fell.

"Okay!" Celia stood up. "Okay then, let's end this. We'll prepare a statement and we'll—"

"Ladies and gentlemen!" a voice boomed from the front of the parking lot. Heads turned to the welcome stage, where Libby and Darryl Lasseter stood at a microphone.

Celia realized. This was happening *now*.

"Ladies and gentlemen, the sheriff informed us that they've arrested the suspect from the fairground," Darryl Lasseter announced.

Sighs of relief emanated from the crowd as they gravitated toward the stage.

"Not only that, but they've identified the suspect . . . as Tom Violet! Husband of known Bufferer Patty Violet!"

"What?!" "Tom?!" Gasps shook the fairgoers.

"Now look! Look!" Darryl spoke from the stage, "I'm not your mayor. I'm not a politician, obviously. I'm just a gym owner with a very brave wife who . . ." Darryl held his fist to his lips, fighting tears. "Who's watched our way of life come under fire because of a conspiracy. Who's watched his town turn on itself because of vile rumors. But that ends tonight!" A billowing Rasta flag looped on a projector screen behind Darryl—the local reggae duo, Jamaican Population, was supposed to perform on the welcome stage. Some onlookers saluted nonetheless. "This week . . ."

Darryl's voice shook as he continued, "I've watched our humanity be called into question. But no longer!" Then Darryl brought the microphone close. "Will the so-called witnesses please come to the stage?"

Heads turned in the parking lot. And at the back of the crowd, Molly looked at Celia. "So?" Celia asked. "What are we waiting for?" Molly managed half a nod before Celia took her arm and pushed toward the front.

"Yeah, hey. Jack Harris here." Jack stepped up to the microphone, wiping sweat. "I just wanna say . . . I didn't see anything that night. I was just making shit up. And . . . yeah." A wave of shock rippled through the crowd. Then in seconds, it melted into relief. Shoulders loosened, onlookers exhaled, a nude man in a dog collar regretted his choices.

"You hear that?!" Darryl asked the crowd. "Another witness telling you that these. Were. Lies," he emphasized. "And if you still have doubts, if you still want to question our reality," Darryl went on, "then we have *another* witness . . ." Celia and Molly headed toward the stage. "No. Two? We have *two* more witnesses coming up here to tell you the truth! Come on up! Let's hear it!"

Molly and Celia climbed the stairs and took the microphone from Darryl. It screeched with feedback. "Yeah, hi!" Celia started. "Thanks, Darryl. Thanks, D.L.," she added, trying something. "So . . . yeah, I don't even know how to start this, really." Celia hesitated. Molly looked sick beside her. "But okay. Monday morning, when I said I saw an error message over the town, well . . . I was lyin—"

Then Molly put her hand on the microphone. She turned to Celia. "Don't."

"What are you doing?!"

"We can't do this."

"Can't do—? Molly, I just said 'I was lyin—.' I got out the *L-Y-I-N*. Do you think they're gonna wonder what I meant by that?!" Celia whispered.

"I don't care. We're gonna find proof."

"We tried! There is no proof."

"Then—screw proof! We're gonna figure this out ourselves. Like you said."

Celia watched as Molly held her ground. It touched her, genuinely. But a bittersweet smile crawled onto Celia's face. For all her hope, and all her fight, Celia Berry knew when it was too late. And right now, it was just too late.

"Molly . . ." Celia peeled her friend's hand off the microphone. "It's okay. It will be okay." Then Celia took the mic and stepped away. She was going to end this herself. "The truth is, it was a lie," Celia told the crowd. "*I* lied. I came up with this 'sign from above.' This 'glitch in the heavens.' And to those of you I hurt, or scared, or cost . . . well, all I can say is I'm truly and deeply sorry. I am. I'm sorr—"

BOOM. A blinding light struck Celia. Pure white. She shielded her eyes with instinct. Then the hum of the crowd roared back in.

"*No way*." "Is that it?" "Oh my God, look!" The entire parking lot was suddenly rapt by . . . *something*. Celia squinted, her eyes adjusting enough to see everyone was looking *past* her. Past Molly and the Lasseters. Celia turned slowly, cautiously. And there it was. Projected onto the stage backdrop, where a Rasta flag once flew . . .

ERROR: SKY NOT FOUND

A photo. An actual *photo*. Of an enormous, cosmic error message in the sky. Almost as bone-shaking and awe-inspiring as it was on that night.

"You want proof?!" a voice screeched from within the crowd. A shock wave of bodies shifted, revealing RJ in the center. "Here's your proof!" he yelled. RJ was standing beside the projector, his phone feeding the photo straight to it. Cold hard proof.

Libby turned to her husband, rage in her eyes. "You said they didn't have anything," she muttered through gritted teeth. But Darryl just stood cowering at the spectacle. It *was* real.

"Are you kidding me, RJ?!" Celia laughed giddily from the stage. "You had a picture?!" She looked at him in amazement. "This whole time you had a picture?!"

RJ smiled, proud as hell.

"Why didn't you tell us?" Molly half yelled.

RJ gave a coy, cool shrug. Then his finger slipped off his phone screen, the photo zoomed out, and an eighteen-foot ghost-pale penis consumed the projector screen. The crowd shuddered. Horrified. "Oh my GOD!" "Is that his—?" "Shield your EYES!" RJ's face dropped. A text bar across the photo read: FOR U GAL, BABY. RJ grabbed his phone and quickly zoomed back into the error message. A sight that, as it turns out, was a cosmic photobomb in an otherwise unexceptional dick pic. The crowd exhaled, spared of the monstrous sight.

Then it zoomed back out to the dick almost immediately. "JESUS!"

RJ scrambled. He zoomed back into the error message. Then it zoomed out. Then back in again. A nun in the crowd almost passed out. And Molly loved every second of it.

~

"Careful! Careful. Don't twist it!" Celia walked beside Molly on Main Street, the giant stuffed penguin swinging between them.

"I'm not twisting—"

"You are! His flipper can't take that much rotation!" Celia warned her, laughing.

Molly smiled. It was a quick, eye-contactless smile, but for Celia it was big.

"So . . ." Celia sighed. "Now everyone knows the truth."

"Yup," Molly popped the *P*. "So what are we gonna do about it?"

Celia chuckled. "Well, *you're* not gonna do anything about

it. You're gonna go back to your own life, where there are much scarier problems, I recall someone saying," Celia teased. "And back here, we'll try to find some answers. Some more signs. Find out what all this means."

Molly thought about it. "Well, I'm not leaving for a day or two. So I can help till then."

Celia smiled. "Okay, that'd be . . ." Then she realized. "Wait, no. You're leaving tomorrow."

Molly shook her head. "Nope. A day or two."

"Nuh-uh. You said that two days ago. Which means you're leaving tomorrow."

"A day or two," Molly droned. Celia slowed down, but Molly kept walking.

"Huh." Celia stood there, a thought nagging at her mind. She almost dropped it. But then, "Hey—Molly?" she called out.

Molly continued on, throwing the penguin stupidly high in the air and catching it.

"Molly? . . . How long have you been in town for?"

Molly turned around, not understanding the question. "I'm leaving in a day or two—"

"Right, you said that," Celia answered. "But how long have you been in town for?"

Molly laughed under her breath like it was obvious. Then her brow knitted as she looked for the answer. She couldn't find it. Why couldn't she find it?

"Molly?" Celia walked toward her.

Molly's mouth moved, but no words came out. "I'm not—I don't—"

"Molly? When's the last time you left this place? Can you even remember?"

A wave of concern washed over Molly. She looked up at Celia, her eyes searching, racing. Suddenly a child looking for protection.

"Celia?"

"I know."

"Celia . . . ?!"

"I know." Celia reached out her hand. "We're going to figure this out togeth—"

404 ERROR. TOWN SERVER CRASH. REBOOTING.

Unchosen

Let's face it: Your twenties are *hard*. Being launched into the "real world" without a safety net is one of the scariest journeys you'll ever take. And if you've read a blog or scrolled through Twitter lately, you know it's especially hard for FGKs: former gifted kids. Chances are you know a former gifted kid. Heck, you may even be one yourself! If you're not sure, don't worry. We'll break it down for you with 11 Ways to Tell If You're a Former Gifted Kid. (Number 6 will shock you! Not really. Ha!)

11. You peaked in grade school

First off, peaking early is common among former gifted kids. Feeling like your best days are behind you can lead to anxiety and stress. It's not your fault you *crushed* fourth grade!

10. You feel burnt out

You're still young, but you already feel like you have nothing left to give. "Bust out the video games, and bring 'em to me. I'm staying in bed all day." —a Former Gifted Kid (Wow!)

9. You were told you were special

Maybe you were told you were a great reader! Maybe you were called a "math whiz." Maybe you were approached by a centuries-old wizard who said you were the "Chosen One," destined to protect the Eight Realms from blood-drenched slaughter. Uhh, hello? Has anyone heard of "kids being kids"?!

8. You had too much pressure on you

"Bring home the A+, Matt!" "Ace the test, Lucy!" "Study the mystic arts to stop reality from crumbling to the Night Phoenix, Dylan! He devoured your parents and he'll come back for you too!" Let's check ourselves before we say *these things* to kids again, K?

7. You failed to live up to expectations

Let me guess. You *weren't* a doctor by age twelve? You *couldn't* cast the Concealment Charm to ward off the Death Reapers from that village? Life is hard! Besides, those kids would've probably been soul-smashed anyway. (You did your best! Self-love is key.)

6. You wish you could relive your childhood

Thing is, you can't. Because you suck at time spells. It's one of the reasons Master gave up on you so quickly. It doesn't matter if his new apprentice is already summoning paradragons. The most you can do is open a void between Rite Aid shifts and scream "Fuck Spencer" into it. "Fuck you, you twelve-year-old, dragon-summoning fuck!"

5. You have migraines

That's gifted-kid burnout for ya! Or maybe that's just your mind link with the Night Phoenix. (If you're teleported to a dark bog with your parents' souls shrieking around you, you're definitely a former gifted kid lol.) Just ignore the bad dreams and go back to smoking Elf weed. You can't get soul-smashed without a soul!

4. You're highly introverted

Do you refuse to make plans? Do you shoot down all the mail owls with your crossbow? Maybe you even cast an invisibility spell on your door to avoid guests. *Knock, knock.* Guess someone got around the spell! But you don't care; you're gonna ignore it anywa—*knock, knock.* Who the hell?

3. You don't want to help others

Classic former-gifted-kid problem. Master's current apprentice comes to your door asking for help, and you don't even want to lend a hand! Even if he says the fate of the Eight Realms depends on it. *Psh.* You're not gonna go out of your way to help some twelve-year-old fuck. Sorry, Spencer! Light this blunt with your dragon fire and maybe grow some pubes on your way out.

2. You experience emotional swings

What do you mean Master is dead? How is that possi— he's supposed to be immortal. If you're a former gifted kid, chances are *this* news will rock your world. But it doesn't matter. It's not up to you to help some kid with his dumbass virgin quest. Besides, you're not "master" material anyway. *Hits blunt.*

1. You learn that being special is a choice

Sooo Spencer's a little shit. He's going off about how you were "never the Chosen One." How he heard you were "a crap apprentice" and "couldn't do time spells for dick." Wow. Future burnout alert! But then Spencer gets quiet. He opens a portal and stares into your unsmashed soul. He tells you that maybe you were never special. But maybe you can be. Maybe you can help him save a world that he still cares about. Why? Because he believes in you. Not in who you were, but in who you might become. Your breath catches. You look into his eyes. You glance at the crossbow on your wall.

You grab your cloak. You step through the portal.

You choose yourself.

Bits & Pieces

REVIEW: *One (Last) Night on Earth*
by Thomas Chisholm

Here's a sentence you've been dying to hear: Live comedy is back in New York. Or should I say, the smoldering, glowing rock heap that used to be New York. *One (Last) Night on Earth* is a variety show tailored tip-to-toe to these nuclear end-times. But will it bring the population back? Don't hold your breath.[1]

Written and presented by Jonah Prett-Lawson, *One (Last) Night* is variety entertainment like the kind you grew up on. (Think more James Corden and less *Amazon Presents: This Robot Ate Jimmy Kimmel's Brain Stem and Does Jokes Now.*) But does Prett-Lawson's romp effectively distract from the radioactive disaster that decimated 99.2 percent of humanity? Let's just say he could've eaten some more brain stem.

---

1 This is a joke. The toxic fumes are more prevalent than ever, and you should, of course, hold your breath.

But let's rewind the tape, shall we? Initially conceived of last nuclear winter, *One (Last) Night* started with an idea. Namely the idea that "Jonah's pretty funny. Not the most funny, but the funniest person left? Maybe?" And suddenly, it was all eyes on former greeting-card writer and occasional meme-reposter Jonah Prett-Lawson.

In a recent interview barely heard over ham radio, Prett-Lawson said that he "hoped to bring some joy" to our vast, infernal wasteland. "Imagine *Saturday Night Live*," he said, "but if your mom just died. And if your friends' moms just died. And if your friends died too." Sounds like regular old *SNL* to me. (Zing!)

But come time for curtains, I can't say I felt that same vision. Prett-Lawson's opening musical medley served as a harsh reminder of the mass death of all professional songwriters on Earth. His monologue, though topical, lacked the joie de vivre needed to distract the audience from the "default thought" (the thought that if you're not already dead, you probably have a new, radioactive appendage growing somewhere that makes you wish you were dead). A far cry from the uplifting yet incisive and ultimately world-saving comedy that we need right now, wouldn't you agree?

Fortunately for viewers, things took a sharp turn with the first guest. Prett-Lawson and his producing team weren't afraid to frontload talent, and out came Jenna Boxer for some lively chat and banter. For those of you who live under a rock, Jenna Boxer is the most famous remaining member of the human race, best known for looking sort of like Kathryn Hahn. Also for those of you who live under a rock: call the Civilian Support and Rescue Hotline if you need food, water, or help getting out from under debris.

The boldness of the *One (Last) Night* booking department continued to shine from there. Other guests included: That Man Who Can Juggle, That Man Who's Learning How to Juggle, a bunch of rats in a trench coat, and of course, the reanimated corpse of Ed Koch. The rats stole the show—no surprise there—with a '30s-esque pratfall routine that proved the time-tested truth that laughter is the best medicine.[2]

Now, if you're looking for more plaudits, I suggest you stop reading here. Because after the novelty of seeing non-exploded humans for the first time in months wore off, the flaws in the enterprise began to show. An eight-hour "In

2 This is a figure of speech. The best medicine continues to be Rexydexy-drecimine, meth, and Aloe for Nuclear Burns.

Memoriam" failed to include most people I knew or cared about, or maybe they were there and just too small to see. And although third-act flooding can't be directly blamed on the producers (broken dams and the burning ocean take that honor), Prett-Lawson's emotional breakdown of "Why?! Why God?! Why can nothing be good, you sick, heartless fraud?!" was hardly reassuring crowd work. But perhaps most troubling of all, the variety show—for all its highs and lows—failed to change the fact that times are depressing and I am depressed. Also they sang "We Are the World," which was bad.

So if you're thinking of seeing *One (Last) Night on Earth*, here's the bright side: You can't. It was a one-night-only event and all the rat-talent died in the fire-floods. But if you're thinking of stepping up to be the next Jonah Prett-Lawson and attempting to bring some laughs to this sprawling death desert, here's a suggestion: Make it funny. And I mean *funny* funny. I've got a glowing tail-arm growing out of my back that I'm really hoping to stop thinking about.

2/5 stars

Our Musings on Comedy
(Vs. What We Pitched)

One of the unexpected side effects of our jobs is that we're sometimes asked to give talks or Q&As. We get asked questions on comedy, its role in society, how we want to contribute to the dialogue, and in response we do our best impression of thoughtful people. So we thought we'd put some of our answers here, along with the sketches we pitched as actual late-night writers that best exemplify our responses.

ON THE ART OF COMEDY: "First and foremost, comedy writing *is* an art form. Like painting, it has brushstrokes. Like sculpture, it requires volume. And like a true masterpiece, just one idea can change the course of history."

WHAT WE PITCHED: Fartbox with Jason Bateman

ON IMPOSTER SYNDROME: "New workplaces are daunting. You'll wonder if you're good enough. You'll doubt whether you belong.

But great comedy is great comedy is great comedy. And creative ingenuity is the ultimate equalizer."

WHAT WE PITCHED: Ice Cube and Ice-T Have a Snowball Fight

ON POLITICAL COMEDY: "Comedy is inherently political. Every joke is a rebel cry, every comedy show a revolution. As humor writers, it's our duty to punch up and never down. To spark discussion. To change the world."

WHAT WE PITCHED: Bernie Sanders Stuffs Ten Peeps in His Mouth and Raps Lizzo

ON FEMINIST COMEDY: "As a male-female comedy team, we have a responsibility, nay, a *responsibility*, to portray women in powerful roles. There's nothing funnier than a woman with great material, deeply complex and rich with nuance."

WHAT WE PITCHED: Constance Wu Bitches Out Your Mom

ON COMEDY AS HEALING: "If laughter is the best medicine, then a comedy writer is the dedicated physician. We heal those who walk through our doors without prejudice or personal gain. Our ideas, like elixir, stir the body to improve, to rise, to survive."

WHAT WE PITCHED: Joe Manganiello Cracks an Egg in His Ass Cheeks (Long Version)

ON PC CULTURE: "Society draws boundaries. The comedian's job is to explore the edges. To be surprising yet sensitive, inventive yet thoughtful. We push the envelope, and yet always—above all else—remain respectful."

WHAT WE PITCHED: Saoirse Ronan Plays "Guess the Jew"

ON SOCIAL MEDIA COMEDIANS: "Come one, come all. TikTokers. YouTubers. Twitter celebrities. But once you get here, you better bare your soul. You better transcend the confines of your phone screen and make yourself heard. Because this? *This* is television. And we don't mess around."

WHAT WE PITCHED: Mr. Beast Tries All the Oreo Flavors—Facebook Watch Exclusive

ON MENTAL HEALTH AND WRITING: "Comedy writing is an endurance sport. Take breaks to let your mind rest. Nourish your health, and prioritize sleep. Burnout is real, and if you're not careful, your ideas could pay the price."

WHAT WE PITCHED: Scarlett Johansson and Andrew Rannells Roll Out on a Piano But Hear Us Out It's Not a Musical But More of an *Homage* to Musicals, She's in a Tux But It's Not Like a Normal Tux and That Is When It Becomes Social Commentary, What's That? Go Home? Our Clothes Smell and Our Eyes Were Closed for That Entire Pitch? Yuh-huh, Got It, Thanks, See You Tomorrow, Jimmy

Welcome to the BuzzFeed Orgy

You'd never describe me as a "wild child." I stayed in for most of high school, studied through college, and the one time I went to Medieval Times, I drank expired mead and had to be walked home by the Green Squire. Parties and I just don't mix. So when Kayla, the office temp, invited me to her friend's house for a night of "group action," I must've lost myself in the hole of her gauge piercing because without hesitating . . . I said yes.

Now, I had heard about parties like this. It starts with a dozen or so twenty-somethings standing around a sublet. They make small talk about restaurants and climate justice and how HAIM's not what they used to be. But eventually, it devolves into what everyone really came for: a night of careless, thrilling, penetrative character reduction. A guy at my gym said he went to one and had three girls at once telling him which *Friends* character he would be. My stomach was in free fall knowing that in a matter of hours, I might be described that succinctly.

At risk of oversharing, I'm no stranger to reducing myself when I'm alone. I've been doing it since I was thirteen, often with the help of the internet—BuzzFeed quizzes and the like. But other times I just used my imagination. I also did it twice in college with a foreign girl who had a thing for reading horoscopes between classes. But what would it be like to be defined by an entire group of people? With everyone watching? The thought of it seemed primal.

Next thing I knew, I was inching down the stairs of Kayla's friend's basement. The musk of humans reducing other humans transported me back to sixth grade, when I horrifically walked in on my parents taking a Which Disney Villain Are You? quiz together. A chill ran down my spine—I thought about turning back. But then I saw a scene that electrified my soul.

In the dim lavender light, clusters of dripping, sweaty party-goers passionately summarized one another for all to see. The basement was bare except for a single velvet couch where a petite blond girl writhed as eight guys told her what kind of *Bachelor* contestant she'd be. (The consensus: a bad one.) In the corner, Kayla the office temp had paired off with a short Italian man who was sensually circling her birthstone. Apparently, he was doing something right, since after each guess, Kayla kept screaming, "No, but I could see how you'd think that!"

But most captivating of all was a stunning brunette leaning against the wall next to me. Her arms were wrapped around this absolute Adonis who knew the Myers-Briggs test and was giving it to her hard. He finished, and she let out a cadenza of moans: "E. N. T! J!!!" Then she smiled and receded into the guy's INFP arms. All I could do was pick at a hangnail and think about how I could never make my partner scream with such a strong sense of self.

"What do we have here?" To my amazement, the brunette was calling out to *me*. "Aren't you just a Ravenclaw-Hufflepuff hybrid?" My legs went numb. Her shimmering eyes came into view as she straightened up. "Oh, wow." Then she leaned into me and whispered, "Go off, Taurus."

I'm a Pisces. But regardless, my head was spinning from such a forward read on my personality. The brunette whisked me away to a private room and threw herself onto a twin bed. "Describe me, Taurus!" she demanded, unbuttoning my shirt. "Describe me in a way that I can easily digest!" *Holy shit*. I caught my breath, then made a clumsy effort to satisfy her with a yearbook superlative: "Most Likely to Take Over the World," I offered, trying to sound assertive. "That's who you are." She cocked her head like it didn't ring true. (In fairness, I would later learn that she had a cousin who died trying to take over the world. Just bad luck, really.) I tried to recover by stepping back and seeing her aura color. But that didn't work either—it was too dark and the only color that came to mind was "doodie brown."

"Enough beating around the bush," she insisted, tossing me down and mounting me. "Reduce me to an adjective, baby."

I hesitated. "One adjective?"

"Yes! Give it to me!" she yelled, unzipping my pants. "One word!"

Then instinct took over. "You're . . . gahh!"

"JUST SAY IT!"

"You're VIBEY!" I blurted. An eternity passed. *Fucking "vibey"?* She slowly rolled off me, and we avoided each other's gazes.

"The last person I was with called me 'outgoing.'" I looked over to catch her scooting off the bed. "I liked 'outgoing' better." And in an instant, she disappeared into the party, leaving me on the damp mattress to analyze myself.

I left Kayla's friend's apartment soon after my disastrous one-on-one, piling into an Uber Pool without so much as rebuttoning my shirt. As I sat there, naked in the rideshare, I caught a glimpse of my reflection in the spider-cracked car window. And oddly enough, I felt more seen than I had all night. There I was, refracted into pieces, staring down a hundred versions of myself. The truth is, I realized, we are all made of one thousand infinities. Of endless, irreducible multitudes. We are not meant to be simplified. Not meant to be lessened. In that carpool cathedral, I simply existed. I was fully me.

But of course *I* would have a deep thought like that. I'm a Ravenclaw-Hufflepuff hybrid.

the end

Easter Eggs

It's Twenty-Twenty-Something, and what good is a piece of media if it's not brimming with subtle hints and references to other pieces of media? Even this very book has hidden Easter eggs that you may have stumbled upon during your read. In case you missed them, though, here's a comprehensive list of all the Easter eggs you'll find in Naked in the Rideshare. *Kevin Feige, eat your heart out.*

1. Page number 1 is a direct reference to how many people Rebecca slept with before Ben.

2. Page number 4 is a direct reference to how many people Rebecca has slept with since Ben.

3. In the background of every scene is an implied Jimmy Fallon Funko Pop.

4. Unless stated otherwise, all the stories take place in Paramus, New Jersey.

5. If you read closely, "Clarity" is about the American TV franchise *The Bachelor*.

6. The chapter "Eustace, 1 Through 84" has three jokes about masturbation, signifying the sacred number 3 (Holy Trinity, Wise Men, cameras on an iPhone Pro, etc.).

7. Zoe from "My College Friend the Pope" and David from "Fairy God Milf" fucked once. Also, Belinda from "Fairy God Milf" fucked everyone in every chapter more than once.

8. The "Coreys" aren't based on anyone we know so much as they are based on everyone we know.

9. Tiny Courtney went to the sleepaway camp from "Letters from Color War" and she fucking loooved it.

10. The "Sky Not Found" character Ellen is a reference to the time Ben interned on the Warner Bros. lot and got the shit kicked out of him by Ellen DeGeneres.

11. Diptyque candles are mentioned once explicitly and forty-eight times implicitly in a bid to get them to sponsor us.

12. The only truly autobiographical chapter is "How to Assemble Your First Couch, You Big Fucking Loser."

13. If followed closely, the steps from "How to Get into the Club" will get you into Soho House and Ludlow House, but not DUMBO House :(

14. Page number 68 is a direct reference to the authors' favorite sex act (almost getting to 69 and then giving up).

15. By connecting all of the *e*s in the book with one unobstructed line, you will have wasted your time.

16. This book serves as the intellectual property for Hasbro's forthcoming *Bop-It* movie.

17. All jokes that don't land for you, the reader, are actually inside jokes that you weren't supposed to get anyway.

18. The aforementioned Easter eggs are all Jewish.

How'd We Do?

Wow, guys. Now that the book is over, we can finally take a step back and reflect on what a beautiful process this has been. We love this book. We're so grateful we got to write it. And ultimately, that's what matters most here. Our pride in our partnership. Our gratitude toward the work. Our challenging, stimulating, fruitful creative journey.

But also, how'd we do?

Did you like it?

Do you like *us*?

What were your favorite jokes?

More important, did you hate it?

Do you hate us and everything we're about?

If so, email us at feedback@rebeccaandben.com. We'll read everything and respond to you in minutes.

Because as much as we can pretend our self-worth is innate and *blah blah*, fill in the blanks—we want to know how *you* feel. Do you like the way we look? Anything you'd change with surgery, temporary or otherwise? If there was a fire, which of us would you save first, and why is it Rebecca?

Are we being clear enough here? Our sense of self hinges on this collection. We hope you laughed, but most of all, we hope we came across as likeable, worthy people. And if this plea for validation comes across as unlikeable and unworthy, please mention that as well to feedbackonthefeedback@rebeccaandben.com.

God, what a roller-coaster ride. Writing. Storytelling. Trying to convince a nation that you're straight-up chillers. If you want to hang out with us, and we're not kidding, all you have to do is ask. If you want to bully us online, and we're again not kidding, our Facebooks are under our real names and we will photograph ourselves crying for you.

Anyway, we love you. We're thankful for you. But mostly we just hope you love us. Thanks for reading. See you next time.*

*If you want to see us next time. We're also willing to retire based on even the slightest criticism.

Love,
Rebecca and Ben

Acknowledgments

We'd like to profusely thank the following people, in no particular order.

Thank you to Blair Kohan, who has believed in us again and again, most recently when we said, "We want to write a book." You changed our lives and are, in fact, The Dream-Maker.

Thank you to Pilar Queen and Dan Milaschewski, who travel near and far (respectively) to celebrate this book with us. Your business savvy is exceeded only by your decency and humor. Thank you for your keenly honed eye for what's funny and, more important, what isn't.

Thank you to our team—Allan Haldeman, Geoff Morley, Danny Passman, and Luke Murphy. We have just, like, 437 more questions for you guys. Thank you for always knowing the answers.

Thank you to everyone at HarperCollins and William Morrow, especially our editor, Mauro DiPreta, who read our deranged stories with an open heart and brilliant mind. Plus a huge thank-you to Elle Keck for taking a chance on this weird, wild collection in the first place.

To Elle Sweeney, Rachel Savage, Zoe Prince, Sari Eichenblatt, and many more for your thoughtfulness, brightness, and support. And to Georgie Koepke for being at the pool party.

To all our teachers who showed us the power of words, especially Ms. Drayer, Ms. Kakounis, Dr. Kelly, Ms. Neuwirth, Mrs. Scarlata, Dr. Schiller, Betsy Paluck, Camille Thomasson, and Ryan Wepler.

To our parents for encouraging us to pursue our dreams. Please accept our gratitude in lieu of master's degrees.

To Lindsay, Adam, Adam, Jacob, Zack, and Morgan. You were the first to make us use humor as a defense mechanism. Thanks? And to Jack, Kenzie, and Ellie: we hope (and fear) these stories will make sense to you one day.

To Jimmy Fallon, who gave us our shot. It's the greatest honor to be on your team, now and always.

To Nick Kroll, Alicia Van-Couvering, and Karey Dornetto. We love you sickos.

To Jessica Elbaum, Alix Taylor, Brittney Segal, Julia Bersch, Allison Silverman, and Will Ferrell for being our creative mishpachah.

To Mindy Kaling for giving Rebecca the best advice of her life: that the kindest, coolest people are the ones who do comedy.

To Marci Klein. We quite literally don't know where to start. Actually, we do. We'll order the edamame.

To everyone who took a chance on our writing up to this point, including the brilliant Amy Solomon, Chris Monks, and the team at *The New Yorker*.

To Valerie Bodurtha, Gillian Bolt, Jacob Clemente, Isabella Giovannini, Jasdeep Kaur, AnnaElise Morello, Sam Uzbay, and the rest of our friends, who moonlight as a brain trust of taste and creativity. Without all of your love, support, and mortifying anecdotes, we couldn't have written these stories. Thank you, and sorry about that thing we said we wouldn't tell anyone. It's in the book in a big way.

To our favorite creative geniuses, David and Shaun Menchel, who helped us crack countless essays in this book. We are endlessly grateful for your minds. Thank you for giving Ben a childhood where making things was the only thing.

To Willie and Norman, for all of the joy and laughter.

And to Milo, a very good dog with a very limited sense of humor.

About the Authors

Rebecca Shaw and Ben Kronengold are a comedy writing team based out of New York. After their college graduation speech went viral, Rebecca and Ben were hired as sketch writers on *The Tonight Show Starring Jimmy Fallon*. Now they write TV shows and movies together, mostly from the same bed, Willy Wonka grandparents -style. Their work has been featured in *The New Yorker* and *McSweeney's*, as well as at that one Bushwick party that turned out to be a sex thing.